EVERYTHING TO LIVE FOR

SUSAN WHITE-BOWDEN

POSEIDON PRESS NEW YORK

A Poseidon Press Book
Published by Pocket Books, a Division of Simon & Schuster, Inc.
Simon & Schuster Building
Rockefeller Center
1230 Avenue of the Americas
New York, New York 10020
POSEIDON PRESS is a registered trademark of
Simon & Schuster, Inc.
Designed by Irving Perkins Associates
Manufactured in the United States of America
1 2 3 4 5 6 7 8 9 10
Library of Congress Cataloging in Publication Data
White-Bowden, Susan, date.
Everything to live for.

1. White, John O'Donnell, 1960-1977.   2. Suicide—
Maryland—Biography.   3. Youth—Maryland—Suicidal
behavior—Case studies.   I. Title.
HV6548.U52M38   1985   362.2 [B]   85-12126
ISBN 0-671-55732-7

SPECIAL THANKS

TO JACK BOWDEN

who gave me the support and encouragement necessary
to write this book and was the first to read and edit it

DEDICATION

To my daughters, Marjorie and O'Donnell, who have suffered more emotional trauma and tragedy in their young lives than most people do in a lifetime and yet have had the courage and strength to go on . . . finding happiness for themselves and providing joy for me and others

How do I begin? How do I speak, feeling such pain? How do I find the words and ignore the tears flowing out of my eyes onto my lips? How do I overcome the lump lodged in my throat? I must, somehow. I must answer the whys in my heart and mind. I must tell this story in the hope that it won't become your story also.

PROLOGUE

HE freshly dug grave looked like an open wound in the lush green pasture dotted with little yellow buttercups. Spring is a time to begin life, not to end it.

It all seemed so wrong and so terribly, terribly sad.

Jody was in the springtime of his life. He was just seventeen. He had everything to live for—or so it seemed to those of us standing around his coffin.

Why had he done it? Why had this very bright, very good-looking, sensitive teenager killed himself?

We all loved him. Look at the tears on everyone's face. Didn't he know how much we loved him? How much we cared and what pain his death would cause?

Why did Jody White do this to us? Why did he do it to himself? Why did he commit suicide? Why did he give up on life, on us?

What happened to the hope and promise his life held when it began?

How did we fail the child whose birth had made us so happy?

Which one of us had the answers locked painfully inside? One of us—or perhaps all of us?

I looked around at our family and friends—at the teenagers, solemn, silenced by the sudden loss of someone who was not supposed to die. Grandparents die, not friends. I looked at Jody's girl friend. This breakup was final. I looked at Jody's sisters—why would he leave them with this pain?—at Jack, who would never know if he could have been a stepfather to Jody, if he could have made a difference.

I looked at the crumpled, tear-soaked tissue in my hand. No one could have loved a child more than I loved Jody. Why wasn't that love enough to keep him alive?

No one knew the answers to the questions. No one really understood. Some had ideas about why it had happened, but no one knew for sure.

The truth of suicide dies with the victim. The survivors can only guess. They must put the pieces of a life together to try to come up with reasons for an unreasonable death.

Certainly the master key to unlock the mystery of Jody's death must lie with me, his mother, and in the soul of a person not standing at the graveside, his father.

CHAPTER 1

THE BEGINNING

MARCH 8, 1960

"*ERE'S* your beautiful baby boy, Mrs. White. Have you picked out a name for him?"

The nurse put my third child in my arms. I looked down at the neatly wrapped baby. All I could see poking out of the hospital receiving blanket was his little round face. I smiled at him.

"Jody, I'm going to call him Jody," I answered. He would be named after his father, John O'Donnell White, Jr., but I would call him Jody. If you say his initials real fast, J.O.D., it comes out "Jody." I loved the boy in the book *The Yearling,* and I wanted my Jody to be just as strong and sensitive and caring about people and animals.

"Well, good luck," the nurse said. "I'll leave you two alone for a while so you can get to know each other."

When the nurse left the room I put my baby down on the bed next to me and carefully unwrapped the blanket to check his arms and legs and to count all his fingers and toes. I talked to him and cooed at him. He opened his eyes, and even though doctors say babies can't see right away, I know when he looked into my eyes he saw me. I smiled and so did he. I felt so close to Jody from that first moment, so much a part of him.

I tickled his little feet. He kicked his legs and moved his arms. He had lots of dark blond hair that I knew would turn to the palest gold, just as his sisters' hair had done. His eyes were what I came to call "Irish tweed"— my hazel color with flecks of his father's bright blue. He was perfect. I even undid his diaper to make sure he was a boy. After two girls everyone was hoping for a boy. I didn't really care, but I knew John would be a lot happier about having a third child if it was a boy. He had wanted a boy with each of the other pregnancies.

I was trying to wrap Jody again just the way the nurse had brought him to me—which is an almost impossible job for anyone but a nurse—when a hospital volunteer knocked on the door and came in. She had the biggest bunch of long-stemmed red roses I'd ever seen.

"Somebody is awfully glad that this baby was born," she said as she put the flowers on the bedside table. There were three dozen roses, one dozen for each child. I knew who they were from even before I opened the card. John was always flamboyant with his gifts. His presents were given to impress, me and everyone else who saw them. I opened the card. It read, "To the mother of my son, Love, John."

"They're from my husband," I told the volunteer hovering close by the bed to see who would be so extravagant as to send three dozen roses. He impressed *her,* I thought as she walked out of the room.

I picked up Jody and, hugging him close to my breast,

got up and went to the window. He may be your son, I thought as tears filled my eyes, but he is my baby. He's been mine alone up until now, and he'll go on being mine.

The bitterness of the past months swept over me. The roses angered rather than pleased me. How could John think that even a thousand roses could make up for the way he had treated me during the past nine months?

John hadn't wanted this baby. We already had the two children *he* had planned for. A third child was more than he figured we could raise properly. "Properly" for John meant private schools, fine clothes, nice vacations; also, we would need an addition on the house. John didn't believe children should be a financial drain on a family. He felt that a couple shouldn't have any more children than they could afford to bring up in the manner in which *they* wanted to live.

When I found out I was pregnant for the third time in four years, he was furious. I had gone against his wishes. Since I was the one responsible for the birth control, it was my fault. I'm sure if abortions had been legal and easily obtained at that time, I would have gotten one to make John happy. As it was, he suggested that I try to find someone who would do an abortion illegally. I couldn't bring myself to do that, and, as a result, my husband, the father of my child, did not touch me and barely spoke to me throughout the entire pregnancy.

I looked down at my baby and hugged him tightly. He was my baby. Whatever I had endured was worth it. Jody was special. I could feel it as he lay in my arms staring up into my face, with eyes that were only hours old. He didn't cry like most newborns in the intervals between sleeping. There seemed to be a peacefulness about this child. I held him close and promised him my love forever. I would show

him how wonderful life could be. We would do things together, go places; we'd share each new experience. I'd be
so proud of this little boy. I just knew he was going to be
handsome and smart, and he would certainly have my un-
tiring, undying love. This baby would have everything to
live for. In that hospital room that first day of Jody's life I
vowed to make that come true.

*The promises we make to our children, our hopes and
dreams for them, are not always easy to fulfill. But I tried,
I really tried, with Jody, with all three of my children. I
wanted the best for them, and for that reason I pushed the
hurt aside. I let my love for my husband resurface so that
we could go on without lingering bitterness or resentment
on my part. I was hoping we could heal our marriage and
start anew.*

*I wanted us to be a family. I wanted the kids to grow up
in a home where their parents loved each other and loved
them. I think what I really wanted was the unreal life I
saw on television during that era.* Father Knows Best *and*
The Dick Van Dyke Show *told me that marriage and
raising children was one continuous situation comedy, a
life that involved lots of love, laughter, and no problems
that couldn't be solved in thirty minutes.*

*When John came to the hospital I thanked him for the
roses and told him how thoughtful he was. We kissed and
he held my hand. The past months were never mentioned.*

*Talking about my feelings with John might have helped
us tremendously, but I didn't do that. I just plunged
ahead, pretending that all was forgiven and forgotten. I
suffered silently, smiled, and acted as if nothing was wrong.*

Jody was everything I hoped he'd be and much, much
more. He was a good baby who never gave me any trouble.
He didn't cry much or demand a lot of attention. He was

content to play in his crib or playpen, allowing me to try to keep up with the needs of his sisters. Marjorie was four when Jody was born and O'Donnell was only seventeen months. The girls adored their baby brother and there was no hint of jealousy. In fact, between the three of us we spoiled Jody terribly—something John tried to stop whenever he saw us doing it. But John wasn't home much. He was very busy in his management job for a large construction company. On weekends he spent a lot of time at the airport flying or working on his private plane, so I was left to take care of the kids pretty much on my own, which gave the girls and me lots of time to spoil our baby.

We would always be there to give Jody whatever he wanted. Somehow it didn't turn him into a spoiled, demanding brat. But I do think it caused him to be a late talker, with an early childhood speech problem, because he never had to ask for anything. We supplied his every need before he was even aware of it. I also think that right then, in infancy, he was given a false picture of a perfect world in which you get everything you want. But Jody was such a joy to give to. His smile was my reward and incentive. He was happy and full of life.

For the first couple of years after Jody was born our lives were not much different from those of most young married couples of the sixties. John worked and I stayed home to take care of the children and the house. We lived in the country on my family's ninety-acre farm in a beautiful but isolated location about twenty-five miles from Baltimore. John and I rebuilt the old farmhouse, which was given to us by my parents as a wedding present. We did all the work ourselves. It was a mammoth job—tearing down, rebuilding, and cleaning up. In the first few years of our marriage we spent most of our weekends and nights working on the house. I thought we would never do anything other than work on the house. But John was dedicated to completing the project, which would give us the kind of home that we couldn't otherwise afford. He seemed tireless in his efforts. John was a determined and willful man—persistent, and usually getting what he wanted, not because things came his way easily but because he made them happen. I found that out very soon after I met him.

It seems incredible now, but I fell in love with John the summer I turned fourteen. Though he was eight years older, there was a boyish quality about him that made him seem a lot younger. There also seemed to be less of an age gap because I was very mature for a fourteen-year-old. John's height—five foot seven—also made him seem more a teenage equal and less threatening than a towering six-footer might have been to a young girl.

John was small but powerful. His shoulders and chest had been well developed by the hard construction work he did and by riding and exercising horses. He had worked with horses at his stepfather's riding academy and at the racetrack before he was drafted into the Marine Corps in 1952, during the Korean War. When I first started dating him he wore his brown silky, uncontrollable hair in a fifties crew cut, which set off his Paul Newman blue eyes and impish grin. Even when he wasn't smiling, the corners of his mouth turned up. I remembered my mother saying to me once, "I hope you'll see to it that Johnny's mouth never droops from sadness. He is a man meant to smile."

I fell in love with the boy and was sexually awakened by the man. John showered me with gifts, his constant attention, and words of love. A year and a half later, in January of 1955, we were secretly married. My parents thought we were going to the College Park campus of the University of Maryland for a dance weekend. (John had started school there after his stint in the Marines.) And they believed I was staying with a girl friend in the women's dorm. John persuaded me that our marriage would work, that he loved me more than anyone else ever would. He said he would make sure that I would never regret marrying him. It seemed so important to him and it sounded so exciting—a secret marriage at fifteen.

Almost immediately, on my honeymoon night, I knew I had made a terrible mistake. I prayed that my mother and father would rescue me, that they would help me undo this very adult thing I had done in such a childish way. I decided that when I got home I would tell them that I had gotten married. I wouldn't keep it a secret as I had promised.

As it turned out, Mother and Daddy already knew. Our names had been listed in a small column in the community paper under the heading "Marriage Licenses Issued," and a friend of the family had seen them and called my parents. Daddy wasn't home when we got there, but my mother said he was pretty upset. Mother was beside herself. She wanted to have the marriage annulled and send me away to boarding school, where John couldn't get to me. "Yes," I cried out under my breath. I didn't want to go to boarding school, but I wanted the marriage annulled. However, before I could speak, she went on to explain that that wasn't going to happen. Daddy had convinced her that if being married to John was something I wanted, they couldn't stop me, because I would just run away and do it again.

Daddy had always given me everything I wanted. I was his pet. He thought everything I did was perfect, that I could do no wrong. But getting married at fifteen was wrong, and if he knew that, why wouldn't he undo what I had done? Why was he willing to let another man take over my life at that age? Many of his dreams, as well as mine, would be destroyed. Those were my thoughts, but I said nothing. I still wonder why I didn't speak out and tell them how I felt.

My parents were loving, caring and concerned, but we never talked about problems or pain.

It was my father's way, the way of his people. He came from a family of strong, hardworking Germans who spoke only of their accomplishments, never of their shortcomings. They rarely admitted mistakes. Their implied message was that if you made a mistake, you dealt with it on your own, quietly. That unspoken rule applied to everyone, even to children. If you had something you were proud of, you spoke; if not, you kept quiet.

My father's way was to become my way. My children got the same treatment from me. I unthinkingly adopted the same "good news only" way of communicating with my kids. I was doing what my father had taught me to do. And so it was when I was only fifteen. I had made my bed, and John was in it. I would have to make the most of it. And that's what I tried to do. I felt that I *must* love John, because our sex life was extraordinarily good. But what we didn't have was the closeness that comes from open communication; we seemed to be on two entirely different wavelengths.

For a few years while we were building the house and having the children, I immersed myself in the home and kids. I tried to push aside my dissatisfaction with the relationship between John and me. My life became birthday parties and dinner parties, cooking and cleaning and carpooling. Since we lived in such a remote area, many of my days were spent importing playmates for our kids or taking Marjorie and O'Donnell to their friends' houses to visit. Jody was still a baby, and I kept him with me. I hated leaving the children, especially for any length of time. When John insisted that we go on vacation alone, just the two of us, I was always anxious and couldn't wait to get home. I didn't think anyone could take care of the kids the way I could, and I felt they probably missed me a lot. I always remembered how I hated my parents to go away and how terribly homesick I was when they sent me to camp at age seven. I carried that feeling over into motherhood, believing that my kids were feeling the same way. The kids usually stayed with my parents, who were right next door. After we redid the old farmhouse, Mother and Daddy built a new house on the farm. Up until then no one had lived on the land. It was just property that my mother had inherited from her father.

Now the children always had their grandparents nearby to make their every wish come true. A new dress or special pair of shoes or boots—Ma and Granddaddy never said no. The kids would run next door whenever they wanted a favor or a treat. My mother always had cookies or candy or fresh fruit ready for family or friends. Her happiness has always been in giving to others. Daddy would take the kids on tractor rides with him or simply hold them on his lap as he watched television. Sometimes all three would climb up and fight over Granddaddy's lap space and attention. He had enough of both to satisfy them all.

John's family was also supportive. His mother and step-father had a magnificent country estate about twenty-five miles from us and also a large summer home in Cape May, New Jersey. The children spent many summer weeks in

Cape May, some without us there but with their grand-parents, aunts, uncles, and cousins. But I really preferred to be with the kids and to take them wherever we went, and we started doing just that.

There were winter ski trips to Pennsylvania, Vermont, or Canada. There was even a fly-off vacation in John's plane to Florida and an outer island in the Bahamas. From the vantage point of our relatives and friends it seemed as though we were the ideal family living an ideal life: a husband who was ambitious and hardworking, both on the job and at home; a wife who was considered suitably attractive, certainly dutiful and socially acceptable; three beautiful children, physically perfect, with above-average intelligence and charming personalities.

What made our marriage and our life together far less than ideal was John and me. Though I looked mature, I was a child bride, totally unprepared for marriage and raising children. John was probably less ready for the re-sponsibilities of marriage and parenting than I was. And the conflicts we experienced over raising the children were endless. We agreed on almost nothing.

John wasn't a bad person; in fact, he was a very good person. He could be caring and thoughtful and very gen-erous. But he could also be demanding and set in his ways. He liked to say, "There's a wrong way and a *White* way to do things. In this family we do it the White way." Un-fortunately for Jody, the White way meant controlling one's emotions. John believed what all too many believed then and still do, that boys should not openly display their feelings, at least not in public, that it is unmanly to do so. How often do we hear a parent saying to a little boy, "Be a big boy now and stop crying"? It was the way John was raised. It was the way he would raise his son, "the heir apparent," as he called Jody.

Jody was a sweet and sensitive little boy who cried as easily as he laughed—that is, before John began his mis-- guided mission to change him. As a little boy, a very little boy, Jody would watch a sad movie on television and the tears would run down his chubby little cheeks as shamelessly as they ran down mine. His laugh was an uncontrollable giggle, reminding me of my own uncontrolled laughter as a child in places such as church, where laughter was entirely inappropriate.

"No son of mine is going to giggle like a girl," John had said often, and he would not tolerate his son's crying in public or displaying any type of emotion in front of people outside the immediate family. Even at home, if Jody fell down and hurt himself and cried, John expected him to stop on command. If he didn't, he was punished. Jody soon learned to control his tears, and as for affection, this little boy who loved as easily and openly as he laughed and cried, was taught to withhold the hugs and kisses. If John caught me holding my little son on my lap, hugging and loving him, I was reprimanded and told to put him down before I turned him into a mama's boy or a sissy. Regrettably, I gave in to my husband's wishes. After all, he was the man of the house, the authority, and he must know best.

I had grown up believing that men always knew best and had the birthright to impose that knowledge on their women and children. Man provides, protects, and directs. Woman accepts, serves, and reassures her husband that he is right even when she thinks he's wrong.

It is a way of life that worked for my parents, and I

EVERYTHING TO LIVE FOR

respected and loved what they were. I tried to follow in their footsteps, and I felt guilty when I finally realized that what was wonderful for them for more than fifty years wasn't going to work for me. But I tried. When I went from living under my father's roof to living under my husband's (I thought of my house as John's), I did try to follow my mother's example. I let John not only control me but mold the children.

The girls' individual relationships with their father were as different as the girls were from each other. Marjorie was her father's daughter. She was the firstborn, and she looked like John and his side of the family. She had his bright blue eyes and smiling mouth. She was petite and perky and full of energy, just like her father. Marjorie had inherited all her father's good qualities—and there were many. Not surprisingly, a close relationship developed between the two. They had so much in common, they were so much alike. They'd be up and gone on a Saturday morning before O'Donnell had even turned over in bed. Marjorie sensed early what pleased her father. She enjoyed winning his approval, and she always did. It was harder for O'Donnell.

O'Donnell was built more like me—tall, with a tendency to put on weight if she even looked at a sugary bun. She was artistic and creative, a dreamer and a thinker, slow to get started in the morning. And although not at all a "natural" athlete, she did become a good swimmer, skier, and motorcycle rider—which is all the more to her credit. O'Donnell eventually gave up trying to be close to her father. It seemed she could do little to please him, and as the years passed she decided it wasn't worth the effort. There were others in her life, and so she went in other directions.

Marjorie and O'Donnell, as exact opposites, would often quarrel and fight. Marjorie was the neat one, with a place for everything and everything always in its place. O'Donnell was a bit on the sloppy side. The reasons those girls had for fighting were endless, but Jody could usually think of some way to settle the dispute. If Marjorie yelled downstairs that O'Donnell had taken her favorite belt and left it at school, Jody would offer his belt to Marjorie. He would give up anything of his to bring about harmony or make the rest of us happy. If I stepped in to side with one of the girls, he'd come to me quietly later on and tell me that I should have let them settle it themselves; it was all right for him to try and make peace, but for me to do it meant I had to show partiality. He was wise beyond his years.

Jody's relationship with his dad didn't become close until, as it turned out, Jody was halfway through his life. John first became something more than a rule maker and enforcer with the introduction of motorcycles into our family life. There had been other activities, such as skiing and ice-skating on winter weekends, but the motorcycles became something really special, something John and Jody shared. At first just the two of them were involved.

From the time Jody was about eight years old he had wanted a minibike. John told him to save his allowance, which he did, and that he would help him buy one. When Jody was about ten he got his first minibike, and shortly after that John got a dirt-bike, which he could ride through the fields and cross-country. They rode together, John on his motorcycle, Jody on his minibike. The motorcycles became the thread that finally pulled this father and son together. It was through the motorcycles that they discovered a common interest and each other. It was through the motorcycles that Jody found a way to excel physically and to please his father.

I did come to think, after Jody started racing motorcycles, that John pushed him too hard, but it was something *they* shared, so I tried not to butt in. I didn't always succeed in suppressing those thoughts, however. Once when Jody was about thirteen and had climbed to the top of his youth racing class, he was competing against one of the other top racers. It was just Chuck Hesse and Jody White in this particular race. As hard as Jody tried, he couldn't get in front of Chuck. The two bikes were side by side for much of the race, but Chuck always pulled away, and eventually he won. I thought Jody rode a heck of a race. John chewed him out.

"You weren't turning on the gas at the right time," he said angrily to Jody after the race. "You backed off when you should have given it everything you had."

"The bike didn't have any more," Jody said in a quiet voice, fighting back the tears. He knew tears were the last thing his father wanted to see at that moment. "I had the throttle wide open," he went on, defending his performance. "Chuck's bike is just faster"—Jody gave one last stab at justifying his effort.

"Bullshit," John said in disgust.

Jody rode back to the trailer in the pit area, head down, dejected. He had not only lost but he had also disappointed his dad.

I had stood silently by while John berated Jody. When Jody was gone I lashed out with the anger and tears I knew my son was feeling and fighting. "How could you say those things to him? He rode a good race and you know it. Maybe Chuck's bike is faster. What difference does it make anyway? Jody enjoys racing, and it shouldn't matter if he wins or loses."

John was stunned by my rare outburst but not to the point of being left speechless. "He's not trying his hardest," he yelled. "If I'm going to spend the money for this racing, he's got to do his best. He can do better. He needs to be pushed."

We stood in the middle of that moto-cross racetrack yelling at each other—a thing we almost never did.

"If you don't like the way I treat Jody on the racetrack," John went on, "you can stay the hell away. This is between Jody and me and doesn't involve you."

I did what John suggested; I left the motorcycles and racing to him. It was hard to be shut out of that part of my son's life, but it wasn't hard to turn my back on John's involvement with it. By that time our marriage had been on the rocks for several years. By then we had been separated several times, and I'm not even sure now whether that incident occurred during one of the separations or reunions. Either way, it was merely one more wedge in the gap that would eventually separate us permanently.

By the time Jody was fourteen we were divorced. The divorce was finalized in March, just a few days after his fourteenth birthday. Marjorie was eighteen that month and ready to go on with her own life, so I didn't think the divorce would affect her. O'Donnell would be sixteen in the fall, and she was very involved with school and church activities, so I figured she'd be all right.

Actually, all the children seemed to take the divorce in stride. There had been so many separations and so much turmoil that it was probably a relief to have something settled. I'm just guessing; I didn't sit down with them and ask what their feelings were—maybe because I was afraid of what they'd say, maybe because if they didn't like it I wasn't sure how I would handle it. My eternal optimism, my sugar-coated outlook led me to believe that everything would work out fine just because I was hoping it would.

Jody accepted whatever came along, and he seemed to want me to be as happy as I wanted him to be. I guess that's why I thought he'd make it, no matter what his father and I did with our lives. I thought it really wouldn't matter if the long, hard struggle to try to make our marriage work eventually failed; if I went to work and began giving long hours to the job; if the time I spent with Jody and the girls became shorter and shorter; if I wasn't always there when they wanted to talk or just wanted some company.

As long as I went on loving him—and that was as sure as the coming of spring—I felt Jody was safe and secure and beyond emotional harm. I was one of those who talked about quality time, rather than quantity, with the children. I now think that both are important. When I look back I realize I was living in my own little world of make-believe, where ignorance is bliss and reality never catches up to you.

By the time of the divorce I had established myself as a reporter for a local Baltimore television station. It was sheer luck that I got a job as a reporter at WMAR, Channel 2, bearing out the old cliché about being at the right place at the right time. Channel 2 needed a woman in its news department. Each of the other two network-affiliated stations in Baltimore already had a woman. I had started out doing some part-time reporting for one of those stations. WBAL had taken me on as an "on air" trainee, and I worked there for several months before moving over to WMAR. I had no background or education in journalism; I didn't even have a college degree. I did have some experience in front of a camera, as I had done occasional part-time modeling and had performed in a few television commercials.

In 1967 that limited background was good enough to get me a job at a television station in a top twenty market. Actually, it was my looks and not my drive that got me the job. No one knew what kind of effort I would put into my work when I was hired, but I had what every TV executive at that time wanted in female talent (and many still insist on it today). I was attractive enough to be a model and I had blond hair. Blond hair was a must for most women hired in television news in that era. One day the lighting was off and my hair looked dark on the TV screen. The general manager stormed into the studio saying, "I hired a blonde, goddamn it—I want a blonde on the air." The most important job the studio guys had to do that day was fix the lighting so that the GM would have his blonde back on the evening newscast.

The door had been opened for me, and I didn't care why. I was determined to make the most of the opportunity. I probably worked longer and harder than most of the men in the department. I never turned down an assignment; I was tireless in my effort to show my colleagues, my husband, and myself that I could do it all—be a wife, mother, and top-notch television reporter without asking for special treatment or consideration at home or at work.

I was still married when I started at Channel 2. John said he would "allow" me to work full time only if I continued to fulfill my obligations as a housewife. The children must always be picked up and dropped off at school on time. The house must always be clean and neat, and the laundry must never pile up. I must be ready to prepare a gourmet meal if John brought someone home from the office unexpectedly. (Company or not, we always ate every meal in the dining room.) I must be willing to entertain regularly on weekends. The lawn must be cut once a week, the garden weeded, and I must always pick up the mail.

It sounds ridiculous now, but I agreed because I thought those were my duties as a housewife. I didn't want to shirk my responsibilities to my family, but I did want to work in television. I wanted to accomplish something on my own. I wanted to be somebody in addition to being some-body's wife and somebody's mother. And I did accomplish that, but in the process I became somebody's ex-wife. My career did not cause my marriage to fail, but it allowed me to see another way of life, to experience my indepen-dence. It gave me the self-confidence that I could make it on my own.

I was now doing that, but with it came a whole new set of pressures. Now I had to try and mesh motherhood, a career, and a whole new role for me—being an adult single woman.

CHAPTER 2

THE BEGINNING OF THE END
NOVEMBER 1974

"*F*OR Jack Dawson on sports, Stu Kerr with the weather, reporters Jack Bowden and Susan White, I'm George Rogers—good night from Channel 2 news. I'll be back with an update at eleven o'clock. Until then, we hope you have a pleasant evening."

The bright lights over the news set went out as we took off our microphones, pushed back our chairs, and got up to leave. "Good night, see you tomorrow," I said to everyone and no one in particular.

Jack Bowden and I left the set together, walked across the studio and out the double soundproof doors into the newsroom. I went to my desk and he went to his. I looked up at the clock, even though I knew what time it was. The seven o'clock news always ended at seven-thirty, no matter how much I wanted it to end earlier. I picked up the phone and dialed the number I'd already called twice since five o'clock. I always worried about the kids after school, worried about what they were doing, worried that they would think I didn't care, didn't love them as much as other mothers loved their children—the mothers who didn't work outside the home or the mothers who worked only nine to five, the mothers who weren't pursuing a career in television. I had realized a long time before that a career in television was more than a job, and I constantly wondered whether I'd made the right decision to continue in this field. Was it something I wanted more than I wanted to be a good mother?

The phone was ringing. Where was everybody? Maybe they were next door at their grandparents'. When the children got to be teenagers I stopped getting outside baby-sitters. The kids said they didn't need one, they were almost as old as the baby-sitters. And "After all," I told myself, "my mother and father are right next door most of the time just in case there is any real problem." Still, I worried.

Finally the familiar "hello" ended the anxious wait. The soft, high-pitched, gravelly voice, so much like my own—mine before I worked so hard to lower it, smooth it out in order to get into broadcasting.

"Hi, Jody, how's everything?"

"Okay."

"Why did it take you so long to answer the phone?"

"I was outside putting my motorcycle away."

"Where's O'Donnell?"

"She's upstairs doing her homework."

"What about Marjorie?"

"She's in Monkton at Kimmie's house."

A pause before I spoke the words: "Is Dad there?"

Another pause. "Yes."

"Okay, Jody, I'll be home in about forty-five minutes—okay?"

"Okay," he repeated.

Jody's voice was unusually quiet. He seemed anxious and concerned.

"I'll be there as fast as I can. Okay?" I tried to reassure him.

"Okay, Mom."

As I hung up the phone Jack walked over to my desk. After seven years of working together, maintaining a friendly but purely professional relationship, with neither of us *ever* having the idea that it could be anything else, we had begun dating and had fallen in love.

Jack is a handsome man, with very dark hair and blue eyes. He is not tall—five nine—but he's well built, a man who works out and watches his weight. At the time he was forty-two.

When we first started working together, what I saw in Jack professionally was a good newsman, the best—hardworking, conscientious, dedicated to getting the facts. He would not report anything before he was sure of what he was saying. In broadcast journalism that is no easy task, especially when one is making live reports as events are taking place or immediately after they have occurred. But Jack had gained a reputation for factual reporting that was, and is, respected by newsmakers as well as the viewing public.

Initially what Jack saw in me professionally was the only side of my personality I allowed to be seen publicly—the sunny side. I was an always smiling, positive person who could find something good to say about almost any situation or story. And though my writing and presentation became more serious in later years, I was saccharin-sweet in the early days of my career—much too soft and superficial for Jack's taste. He figured I was probably just as shallow inside as I was on the air and around the station, pleasant but not someone you would want to spend a lot of time with.

With time we did become good friends, and as the years passed, those initial impressions were changed, enhanced, added to and improved. I learned that Jack had a keen sense of humor and was much more prone to outbursts of laughter than to the occasional spurts of anger I'd seen him display over frustrating situations. His laugh is an infectious one, the kind that takes over a room or movie theater or television studio. One can't help smiling even if one doesn't know why he is laughing. With almost a single word or look he could set me off. And he got great pleasure out of doing that, especially when we were on the news set just before air time. He'd love to see me giggle like a little girl and watch the tears form black mascara streaks down my cheeks. Then he'd laugh as I'd frantically try to wipe them away before the camera was turned in my direction.

We had good-natured fun with each other. Our egos weren't so fragile that we couldn't tease each other about our faults and foibles. It was wonderful to relax and be myself with someone. We also developed tremendous respect for each other's work. As I matured in my role of reporter, growing out of what Jack called my "Pollyanna phase," he began coming to me for advice and criticism of his work. He made me feel important. For the first time in my life I felt intellectually equal to a man.

When I think back on it, that on-the-job friendship might have been the only constant in both our lives. In the seven years leading up to our finally dating, Jack married his second wife, had his one and only child, separated from his wife, and got into and out of yet another serious relationship. Meanwhile John and I had undergone several traumatic separations and had finally gotten divorced.

It was against that background that Jack said to me one night, "Look, I'm not seeing anyone right now, you aren't either. Why don't we go out together? You know we'd have fun; at least we'd have a few laughs."

Our first date, dinner after work, was magic. It was just the way it is in the movies. We both knew at the end of that evening that we were in love and wondered how we could have worked together all those years and not felt something of what we were now feeling.

I'd already told the children about Jack. O'Donnell and Jody knew him only from seeing him on the news, when I insisted we watch that instead of their favorite show. Marjorie had gotten to know Jack the previous winter when she interned at the station during her senior year. She liked him, and she knew we were friends, although the thought that it could be anything more than friendship probably surprised her almost as much as it did me. But she was happy for me. What concerned her was what concerned me: her father. She knew John had wanted the divorce when we finally got it. She knew that at the time he was in love with an eighteen-year-old, a woman just a year older than Marjorie.

And Marjorie knew that her father's relationship with that young woman had turned out to be nothing more than a fleeting affair and that now he wanted us to get back together again. That, combined with my starting to see Jack, spelled trouble to Marjorie, who knew how possessive her father could be. I knew this better than she, and it made me uneasy as I thought about it that night in November, standing in the newsroom.

"You look worried," Jack said with concern as he stood by my desk.

"I am," I responded. "John's at the house, and I know it's not going to be a pleasant evening. He just won't leave me alone. He refuses to accept the divorce, and he keeps pushing for a reconciliation. I'm beginning to think he'll always be there, that I'll never have a life without him. He's around every corner. I'm constantly looking over my shoulder, wondering when and where he'll appear next and what he'll do."

"I think you just have to be firm," Jack said gently. "You have a right to your own life, you know."

"I know you're right," I said, "but it's so hard. You don't know how difficult John can be." I looked up at the clock. "I've got to go. I told Jody I'd be right home."

"Please be careful," Jack said, reaching for my hand, "and remember I love you."

"I love you too," I said, forcing a smile to try to reassure him that I'd be all right.

The drive to Carroll County always gave me time to think, to reflect on the events of the day. Most nights I used the time to try to leave the world of television behind, to mull over what had happened that day and then put it to rest. If things hadn't gone right, I tried to push the unpleasant recollection to the back of my mind. I would use the drive home to talk to myself on such nights: "What's done is done. That's live television: you say something you wish you hadn't, you look like a fool for a minute, you wish you could take back what you've said, you wish you could do it over the right way to show everyone that you really are good, that you can be poised and professional and that you're quite ready to replace Barbara Walters. But there's nothing you can do, so forget it. Besides, there's always tomorrow to show everyone you can do a good job."

That's what I like about television news—every day is complete unto itself. It suited me perfectly. It was the way I wanted all of life to be. If a problem can't be solved today, forget it, because it won't be around to worry you tomorrow.

But on this night I wasn't thinking about what I had done during the day. My thoughts returned to John and what lay ahead for me at home. I knew what he wanted, what he'd say. We'd been through it all before. It had been six months since the divorce became final, but now he was insisting that we should try again.

I couldn't and wouldn't go back to that. I wouldn't trade my release from that pain for his or my or even the children's security. There had to be a better life for us all, a life free of deceit, infidelity, and pretense. I had said these things to John so many times, long before Jack meant anything to me. Now I was even surer they were true.

John and I would share the children's lives, but our existences as a man and woman must be separate. I had legal custody of the children, who were living with me on the farm, but he knew I'd never try to restrict the time he spent with them. I couldn't. They were practically adults and had a great deal to say about what they wanted to do and with whom—and they wanted to spend time with their father. I think the separations and divorce brought John and all three of the kids closer together. But even more than the girls, Jody was spending a lot of time with his dad. Many late afternoons and weekends they spent together working on and riding the motorcycles.

John was there many nights when I got home from work; many nights he stayed for dinner. I would never try to limit his time with his kids, but that had to be enough. There couldn't be anything more between us.

For so long we had had an emotional stranglehold on each other. We'd struggle to try to free ourselves, but somehow at the most vulnerable moment one of us always reached out to drag the other back. The tie was insecurity, the love selfish.

And there were always the children, whom we both loved very much.

That's why I decided that I must be firm on this night—no more on-again, off-again relationships. We were divorced; we must, we *had* to go our separate ways. We had all been through enough. The sooner we accepted that the sooner we could get on with the business of living, perhaps even the pursuit of happiness.

I really did think John also needed to go on with his life *without me*. My career and the years of natural maturing had taken me beyond what we had once shared. I no longer leaned on him. In fact, I had stopped being able to tolerate the control and dominance John had been taught to believe was proper, even expected, of a husband. I had broken out of the mold that a well-bred, well-trained wife was supposed to fit into. I couldn't go back, and John could never embrace what I had become.

As I drove up the dirt road that leads to the house I started thinking about all the times when I had resolved to end my marriage but had ended up going back to it. Tonight would be different, I vowed. Our lives couldn't go on this way.

As I turned the corner at the top of the hill, the first thing I saw was John's little red sports car parked where his cars of varying makes and models had always been parked since we first moved to the farm seventeen years ago. I pulled my car in beside his, as I had done a thousand times before. I got out of the car, went down the walk and in the front door. Tonight I must deal with this man. I must face him and somehow help him find a rational, reasonable solution to his problem and mine.

I walked into the den, and there he sat in his big, brown leather chair, to the left of the stone fireplace. He looked so small sitting there, so thin. It had only been a few days since I'd seen him, but he looked so different. His face was drawn and he looked as if he'd lost a lot of weight. He was shaking and he was breathing so rapidly that he almost seemed to be hyperventilating. I asked if he was all right.

"I was until a few minutes ago. Jody said you'd be home at eight-fifteen, and when you didn't get here then, I thought maybe you had gone out again like last night, and I started feeling sick and dizzy. Isn't that silly? But I can't help it. I'm no good without you. I need you."

"John, please don't talk like that. You just need professional help to deal with this." Then I grew impatient, almost angry at his negative attitude, his dependence on me. I felt suffocated. "Why now, all of a sudden? We've been divorced since March. This is November!"

"I thought maybe we'd get back together, like we always have. But you've found someone else now, haven't you?" he asked.

"Yes, I'm dating someone," I admitted.

"Do you love him?" he asked.

"We're fond of each other," I said gently.

"I just can't face it," he said.

"Of course you can. I'll help you find the right doctor to guide you."

"That costs too much money," John argued back.

"We're not poor, and it's money well spent if it helps you get a grip on your life."

"They don't do any good anyway."

He always came back to the same excuse.

"Where are the children?" I asked, changing the subject.

"In the kitchen."

I walked out of the den, through the living room, dining room, and into the kitchen.

"Hi, guys." I tried to be cheery.

The mood was somewhat different in the kitchen. The TV on the counter was on; there was at least noisy activity. Life was going on out there. Perhaps they were taking a page out of my behavior book and pretending everything was all right while their father sat depressed in the other room. Perhaps they were avoiding something they didn't want to face or didn't know how to handle. O'Donnell was sitting at the kitchen table at the end of the room, and Jody was standing at the stove cooking.

"This is a switch. What's gotten into you, my dearest, darling son? You're doing the cooking when your sister is here to cook for you! Couldn't you sweet-talk her into doing dinner for you?"

"No, I thought I'd do it for a change. A guy has to be well-rounded these days, you know."

"I know, but I didn't think you did. I'm glad you've

seen the light." This was highly unusual. Jody never cooked.

I turned to look at my daughter. Her face was troubled and confused.

"What's going on with you and Dad?" she asked.

The past few years had been difficult for this sixteen-year-old, who placed home, family, God, and church above all else. Thank the Lord she had had the church to turn to; her home had certainly provided no solace. Perhaps O'Donnell had turned to religion to help her cope with our unstable home life; maybe it was because she got peace and comfort from her faith that she was able to handle the problems over the years. Whichever came first, it worked; thank God, it worked for her.

"Why couldn't we be like other families?" she had asked. Some of her friends' parents were divorced, but even those broken families had some normalcy about them—but not ours. For the past four years the children had never known from one day to the next if their mother and father would be together or living apart. (I think children can accept anything, any life-style, and adjust very well if there is consistency and understanding. But if there is constant change and they are kept in the dark about the reasons for it, they have no chance to develop any kind of security or sense of family belonging.) One evening, after a period of separation, O'Donnell came downstairs and into the kitchen to find her father and me talking and laughing as if we had never been apart. It was one of those times I was drawn back for physical nurturing, a return to our past when love was all that mattered—and love was sex. She just looked at us in a way that made me feel as though she had caught me in bed with a total stranger.

"Are you getting a divorce or not?" Her tone indicated she wanted the answer to be yes.

"I don't know," I said.

Her father quickly jumped in, saying, "It's none of your business what we do anyway."

She was crushed. Her eyes filled with tears, and she turned and went back to her room.

I let her go without saying anything, not realizing at the time how hurt she must have been, how unimportant that remark must have made her feel. I didn't stop to think about the emotional devastation such a comment can cause a child. I didn't act on my instinct to go to her and comfort her. I sat staring at John in disbelief.

Divorce is not just between a husband and a wife. When there are children, it involves them. Their feelings need to be considered as much or more than those of the adults. I wish I had thought about that then.

O'Donnell never asked about the status of our relationship again. She waited to be told, and then she accepted and tried to cope as best she could. On that night I saw the old fear creeping back into her expression, the fear that it might be happening once more, that we might be getting back together again. But what I told her was just the opposite.

"I've got to make your father understand that there will be no more chances for us to start over again with each other. That is all in the past now."

O'Donnell listened without comment, showing neither approval nor disapproval. I looked at Jody, who had turned to listen. There was no hint in his expression either of what he was thinking. The children had learned much too well to conceal their real feelings.

"I'll be in the den with your father. Just give us a call when your wonderful dinner is ready."

John was still sitting in the same chair, staring into space.

"Do you know that your son is cooking dinner? He knows there are problems between us, and he's dealing with them as best he can by trying to lend a helping hand, trying to make things a little easier for everyone. He's pitching in and making an effort to cope. Can you be less a man than your son?"

"I guess so," John mumbled. "I guess I am."

And then he started to cry. It was only the second time I'd ever seen John cry. The first had been when I was fifteen years old. John and I had been going together for a year at that point. I felt our relationship was getting too serious and I wanted to date other boys, so I broke up with John. He followed me day and night, driving past my house, showing up everywhere—at the swimming club, at the rec center. I couldn't get away from him. One day he asked to talk to me, and I sat in his car as he pleaded with me to come back to him. He started to cry and said he hadn't felt this way since his father died.

"I just don't have the strength to face life anymore—not without you," John was saying now.

"Of course you do," I said as gently as I could, sorry that I had accused him of not being the man his son was.

"No, I don't," he kept repeating.

"Dinner's ready, come and get it!" Jody shouted from the kitchen.

"Come on," I said, "let's go have some of your son's dinner. He's worked hard over it, and I'm sure he's proud of his accomplishment. Come on, it will make you feel better."

As hard as I tried to keep the conversation going at the dinner table, the atmosphere was depressing. The children were quiet, staring at their plates. Jody did look at me several times with a look that asked, "Are you all right?" I smiled back in my reassuring way.

At fourteen Jody had become my protector. In John's absence he was the man of the house. He did chores that a man would tackle. He tried to make life easier for me, and he loved to brighten my day with little surprises. On that night Jody seemed to be on the verge of coming to my defense against his father. I think if I had given him any indication that it was necessary he would have done that. I didn't. My gaze switched to John. He looked so sad, so pathetic. John seemed to have trouble swallowing, even though he did compliment Jody on his cooking. Nobody ate very much. John drank a couple of beers. The whole meal took only about ten minutes to serve and consume.

"I'll clean up," O'Donnell volunteered.

"Good God, what's getting into you children? I don't think I can stand all this willing help."

But, I thought to myself, they sense trouble. They're trying so hard to ease the tension that's filled this house.

"Okay, I accept your kind offer."

I turned to John and said, "I'm going upstairs to take a bath and wash my hair. I have a splitting headache, and maybe the water will help clear my head and my thoughts."

I went upstairs and into the bathroom to start running the water in the tub. As I came into the hall Jody was coming up the steps to go to his room on the third floor to do his homework. We looked at each other, but before we had a chance to speak we heard John's footsteps on the stairs. We turned to watch him as he reached the landing at the top of the main staircase. He took the two last steps, which brought him to where we stood and turned to face Jody. He stared at his son for what seemed like an eternity, but it was really only about thirty seconds.

"What are you looking at?" Jody said kind of harshly to his father.

As he answered, John reached out to put his arms around Jody, to embrace him, as he did so often. The two hugged all the time, something I always resented because I had been denied the right to hug and touch and feel close to my son. It was unacceptable in John's eyes for a mother and son to be physically affectionate, but it was all right for father and son.

As he reached out, John spoke, never taking his eyes off Jody's face. "I'm just looking at you. I'm so proud of you," and he tried to pull Jody into the embrace. But for the first time in his life Jody pushed his father away, perhaps sensing something strange about him on this particular night. Jody rejected the man he so wanted to be like.

John's arms dropped limply to his sides as Jody turned and climbed the stairs to his room without speaking another word. I walked back into the bathroom, closing and locking the door behind me. I just didn't trust John; I didn't want him walking in on me. I wanted to be alone for a few minutes. How was I going to handle him, handle this impossible situation?

I got into the tub and let the hot water rush over my body, slipping down to get my hair wet. It felt good—the water washing through every strand of hair, making my aching head feel a little lighter. I was putting on the shampoo when I heard the doorknob turn. I raised my head to watch it turn again. There was a rattle as the door was pushed, but the lock held it. Then came a knock and John's voice.

"Let me in, please, for just a minute."

"I'll be out in a few minutes," I said.

"I need to see you now. Please. Don't deny me one last thing."

My heart leaped into my throat. What was going through his mind? I got out of the tub, put a towel around me, and opened the door. John stepped into the small bathroom that he had built.

"I want you to kiss me goodbye—and remember, I loved you. I've always loved you."

"What are you talking about? If you're saying what I think you're saying, I don't want you to talk like that. Don't even think such things."

"Just kiss me goodbye," he said, and he leaned forward and kissed me lightly on the lips. He turned and walked out of the bathroom, closing the door behind him.

I went to the door, locked it again, and climbed back into the tub. I just wanted to wash it all away. I wished so much that I didn't have to deal with these problems. But I couldn't push his look, his words, his strangeness aside. Could it be that he was leaving, that I wouldn't have to get into a long discussion that night? That's what I wanted to believe.

What had he really meant? Was he trying to scare me? Was it a threat, an insinuation, once again to make me give in to what he wanted?

My thoughts were interrupted by a loud noise in the bedroom. My heart stopped. It was a gunshot. My heart started pounding. What did it mean? Was he trying to scare me? Was he trying to lure me into the bedroom to kill me? Could he have—? I wouldn't let myself think the words. I climbed out of the tub once again, my hair still foamy with shampoo. I wrapped the towel around myself again, unlocked the door, and walked into the hall. The children must have heard the shot too, but the house was deadly quiet, as if no one were breathing. They too must have been listening, wondering what had happened, what that noise had meant. The door to my bedroom was open. I stepped into the doorway, and there on the bed lay the man who moments ago had been standing in front of me. My God—I clasped my hand over my mouth to keep from screaming. There was a gun in his right hand, the German Luger he kept in the bedside table. My first thought—which burdened me with guilt for months to come—was Thank God it's over—thank God his pain and mine are over.

I walked quietly, carefully into the room and stood by the side of the bed. It was an awful sight, one I'll never forget. There was no movement, and there appeared to be no breathing. I didn't think to take his pulse, and it never crossed my mind to administer first aid. I assumed my husband was dead. He had killed himself.

I walked out of the room and closed the door. I didn't want the children to see what I had just seen. I didn't want them to live with that image of their father. There was still no movement from O'Donnell's or Jody's rooms. They were probably afraid to move.

I walked into O'Donnell's room, which was also on the second floor and fairly close to my bedroom; she had to have heard the shot. She was sitting on her bed with her back up against the backboard, staring at the doorway as though waiting for someone to come through it and explain the gunshot. Perhaps she wasn't sure who would walk into her room. I went to her side, took her in my arms, and said, "Your father has shot himself."

She gasped and started to cry. "Oh, no!" she wailed. "Oh, my God."

"He was so sick, O'Donnell, so disturbed, and he wouldn't get help."

We hugged each other and cried until I sensed someone standing at the door watching us.

"Jody," I said, "oh, Jody, Dad has shot himself."

I repeated what I said to O'Donnell. I put my arms around my son, but there was no response, no tears. Jody didn't speak and he didn't cry.

"I've got to call someone. I've got to call the police. Come downstairs with me."

We all walked down the steps to the kitchen, and thus began a nightmare I thought would never end. *And perhaps it never has and never will. I don't remember who wrote it, but I remember reading that suicide never kills just one person, and that may be the intention of some who kill themselves—to punish—to provide an agonizing existence, even to kill those they feel are responsible for making them miserable, for not giving them their way. Those who are left behind are left not only with grief but with guilt, and I think many who commit suicide are counting on that. It's their legacy if the survivors accept it. What we don't realize at first is that we can reject that guilt.*

Within minutes after I called the State Police the house was swarming with people—policemen, firemen, medics. There were flashing lights, and a helicopter landed in the pasture in front of the house. I couldn't believe this was all happening. I couldn't believe John had actually shot himself. I felt panic and terror racing through my body. My heart was pounding and my temples were throbbing, but I tried to remain outwardly calm for the children. I knew that they must be just as terror-stricken as I was, probably more. As O'Donnell, Jody, and I sat huddled together on the living room sofa, we watched two men carefully carrying their father on a stretcher down the narrow stairs of the old house, giving each other directions in whispered tones.

John's entire head was bandaged, and they were being so careful. My God, could it be that he wasn't dead? I leaned over to the children and whispered words of hope. "Maybe Dad's not dead. Maybe they can do something, maybe they can save him."

They just looked at me; they looked frightened, but they weren't crying and they still weren't saying anything. I put my arm around O'Donnell and reached over to hold Jody's hand. I had called John's brother—he and his wife were on the way to the house—and I had called Marjorie. She had sat up with John the night before when I was out. They had talked; John had done most of the talking. She had listened, accepting his pain as her own, feeling sympathy and taking upon her shoulders the weight of her father's problems, a burden no eighteen-year-old should ever be asked to carry.

She, of course, could offer no solutions to her father's dilemma, and she knew in her heart she couldn't do what he wanted: appeal to me to rejoin him as his wife, make us a family again. She knew how wrong that would be for me, and I think she knew from past experiences that it would be wrong for all of us. But she listened because she deeply cared. This was a man she loved very much. He had been a good father to Marjorie.

O'Donnell and Jody stood next to me in the kitchen as I called their sister. Marjorie was visiting her girl friend Kimmie, who lived about twenty-five miles away. When I called, Kimmie answered the phone, and I asked, as calmly as I could, to speak to Marjorie. My daughter got on the phone, a note of anxious concern in her voice as she said, "Hello, Mom, what is it?"

"Marjorie, you have to come home right now—okay? Drive carefully and don't speed, but I need you right away, okay?"

She didn't question me, perhaps she was afraid to. She said okay and hung up. I knew if I had told her what had happened she would have become hysterical and would never have been able to drive the distance from Monkton to Finksburg safely. Thirty-five minutes later, when Marjorie drove into the driveway, she was greeted by the flashing lights of the police cars. The helicopter, which was taking her father to the Shock Trauma Center in Baltimore, had left, but there were still many people around, including detectives and John's brother and sister-in-law, who had arrived by then.

She pulled her car into the first available space, which was up on the lawn, jumped out, and ran frantically into the house. As she burst through the front door and saw me she started to shout, "What's wrong, what's going on?"

I ran to her, took her in my arms, and said as gently as I could, "It's your father, Marjorie—he's shot himself."

"No!" she screamed at the top of her lungs. "No! Where is he?"

She broke from my clasp and started racing up the stairs.

"Wait, Marjorie—he's not there. They've taken him to the hospital."

I had to stop her before she got to the bedroom. I didn't want her to see the blood and the bullet-smashed window. I ran up after her. She turned at the top of the stairs.

"I want to go to the hospital. I want to be with him."

"I don't know if they're going to be able to do anything, Marjorie, and I don't know what good it will do for us to go there."

"I don't care," she screamed back, tears flooding her face with every outburst. "I don't care. I want to go. Please, I want to go. Please, please, please," she sobbed.

I looked at her uncle Taylor. He nodded his approval.

Even at this moment of intense emotion, as my daughter searched desperately for approval from me, I looked for a male authority to tell me what to say. John was dead or dying, so I turned to his brother to tell me that what we wanted to do was okay.

It was decided that O'Donnell and Jody would go to John's brother's house with their aunt. Taylor, Marjorie, and I would go to the hospital, stopping along the way to pick up John's mother and stepfather.

Shock Trauma at the University of Maryland Hospital is world-famous, and though I had read about it and heard it mentioned in practically every newscast—"The accident victims were taken to Shock Trauma"—I had never been there. Somehow in all my years of reporting I had never been assigned a story that involved coming to this unique medical facility. But I knew of its extraordinary accomplishments in the field of emergency medicine and the miraculous results often achieved by the doctors and through the equipment, techniques, and revolutionary procedures there. I knew if there was any place in the world where someone with such a life-threatening injury as a bullet wound to the head might have a chance to survive, this would be it.

It was with this knowledge—perhaps giving me a false sense of hope, which I passed on to my daughter—that we entered Shock Trauma. We followed the red lines and arrows on the floor leading us through automatic doors, down long hallways, and finally bringing us to a waiting room. We looked around, found someone to ask, and were told, yes, we should wait there. A doctor would come down and talk to us soon. The room was plain—no decorations, no warmth, hard chairs, cold, blank walls. The five of us sat and waited, staring at the walls, at each other, and down at our hands to avoid revealing our real fears. I looked at my mother-in-law—how awful this must be for her! That was her son in there, her son who had shot himself. Did she blame me? Did she blame herself? After all, Taylor, the son sitting next to her, was her favorite. John knew it, everyone knew it. John had been the difficult one, difficult and rebellious.

After what seemed like forever, a doctor walked into the waiting room, a foreign-looking man who had "doctor" written all over him. We stood up abruptly.

"Mrs. White?"

"Yes," I said anxiously.

"Your husband has suffered a severe wound to the head. The bullet penetrated the [technical word] and severed the [technical word], and there was tremendous loss of blood before he got here. Perhaps if—"

I cut the doctor off in mid-sentence. I had no patience for a long, drawn-out explanation. I couldn't listen to any more meaningless words. I almost screamed, "What are you trying to tell me? Just say it, for God's sake."

"Your husband is dead. He died in the helicopter on the way here."

Marjorie started to shout and cry. I took her in my arms and kept saying over and over, "I'm sorry, Marjorie, I'm so sorry."

"It's not your fault, Mom, it's not your fault."

She tried so hard to ease my guilt, to make sure I knew she didn't blame me for the incredible pain she was now feeling. Why, then, did I feel so responsible? If only I hadn't taken a stand that night, if only I had waited—waited until John had found someone else, waited until he was the one who wanted to end the relationship once and for all. What *had* I done?

John's brother talked to the doctor in muffled tones—what to do with the body—cremation—has to go to the medical examiner first. I stood next to my sobbing daughter, feeling so helpless.

Her father was gone and she would never see him again. And there wasn't anything I could do—not any longer. We walked down the halls, this time against the arrows, out through the same automatic doors. We went out exactly as we had come in, except that we no longer carried with us any hope that the life of John White might continue. He had chosen to die. He had accomplished his mission, and now we were left to live with his decision—or to try to.

CHAPTER 3

DAD'S DEAD

I SAT on the bed, looking down at Jody. The light from the hall through the partially opened door fell on his blond hair, creating almost a halo effect. His face was in shadow, and at first I couldn't tell whether he was awake or asleep. But as my eyes quickly adjusted to the dark room, I could see that his eyes were open. He moved his head on the pillow and looked into my face, searching for an answer to the question that I'm sure had been keeping him awake. Was his father alive or dead? I'd already told O'Donnell, who was waiting up for us when we got back to Taylor's house, and now I spoke the words to my son, words that I knew would have a profound effect on him for the rest of his life.

"Dad is dead, Jody. He was dead when he got to the hospital." I put my head down next to his, my hand stroked his hair as I cried on my baby's shoulder. He was fourteen, but he was still my baby. My tears soaked my child's pillow. "I'm so sorry, Jody. I'm so sorry. I'd give anything if it were different, if you didn't have to face this, if it hadn't happened."

I felt so guilty, so responsible. Why hadn't I protected him from this hurt when I'd had a chance?

"I love you, Jody. I need you. We're all going to have to be strong, to pull together."

I touched Jody's face with my fingertips and wiped away his tears. There were tears. I don't know if they were for his father or for himself, but there were tears, if only a few, for a few minutes. I kissed him on the cheek and said, "Try to get some sleep. We're going to make it, Jody. I promise you we'll make it without Dad. It won't be easy, but we're going to do it. We've got to."

I walked down the hallway, checked on the girls again to make sure they were doing okay. Then I crawled into a bed in another room without even taking off my clothes. I closed my eyes and made myself turn off my mind, made myself stop thinking, stop picturing, stop reliving, stop agonizing over what had happened. I wasn't even sure what time it was or how long all this had taken. I had to get some sleep. There would be a whole new set of problems to face in just a few hours.

Sleep came from exhaustion but not for long. It was barely light outside when I awoke with a start. I looked around, realizing very quickly where I was and why.

"Oh, my God," I said out loud. "John's dead. He killed himself, he did it, and there's nothing I can do to bring him back. I might have saved him last night, but there's nothing I can do now."

How could I have been so cold, so uncaring? How could I have let this happen? Good God, what am I going to do? I've killed the father of my children. *If it hadn't* been for me, he would be alive right now. *I* could have saved him—

if I had told him I cared, *if I had* been more understanding, *if I had* taken more time with him, *if I had* tried to stop him, *if I hadn't* been so afraid, so concerned about my own life.

The "if I hads" and "if I hadn'ts" kept coming for me and for the children for many months and years ahead. It's the single most destructive thing that survivors of suicide victims have to cope with. The death causes grief, but the "if I hads" cause incredible and sometimes intolerable guilt, guilt that must be understood, dealt with, and overcome if relief from such a heavy burden is ever to be achieved.

I got out of bed with some difficulty—I was dizzy, and my head ached as if someone had been pounding on it with a sledgehammer. I looked in on the kids. They were still asleep. I went to find some aspirin, and then I went downstairs. Betty, Taylor's wife, was already in the kitchen. She asked if I had slept and how I was. I said a little and not so good.

"Yeah, it just hit me this morning what has really happened," she said. Her voice cracked and tears filled her eyes. She asked if I'd like some breakfast.

I said, "No, thank you." I told her I was sure I couldn't swallow and I just wanted to wait for the children to get up so we could go home.

"You don't want to go back to the house yet?" she asked, shocked that I had even suggested it.

"Yes, as soon as possible. We have to go home sometime, and I think the sooner the better."

"Perhaps you're right, but Taylor and Bill [John's sister's husband] want to go up there and straighten things up."

"I would appreciate that, but as soon as I can, I just want to go home with my children."

I somehow felt that if the children and I could go home, things would be better, we'd feel better. I wanted to start making things "all right" for them. I felt so guilty, so responsible for their losing their father. I wanted to start making it up to them—as if I ever could.

I started to cry, and Betty didn't try to stop me, knowing it had to come out. When the children got up and came downstairs, the pain inside me swelled to a new intensity. Their solemn faces revealed the deep sadness in their hearts. But there was no malice there. They didn't blame me—and they were trying so hard to make sure I didn't think that they did. I asked how they felt, and they said "All right" or "Okay" or "You know." Yes, I knew. I would have given anything to spare my kids that kind of suffering. But it was too late. I couldn't do anything now except try to "make it all better." And in trying to do that, once again I didn't use the most valuable method available—talking to them. I didn't ask what they were feeling or thinking. I didn't share my thoughts with them, so that they could also understand how I felt and how I ached for them.

About eleven o'clock the minister arrived to talk about funeral arrangements. The children and I sat down together to talk to him. He was a kind, compassionate man in his early thirties, and I had always thought that for someone so young he showed enormous caring and understanding. I suppose one ages and matures quickly when faced with human suffering and tragedy on an almost daily basis. Some people exposed to the misery of others manage to keep it from touching them, but not this man. Not only does he physically reach out to touch you when he greets you and talks with you, his eyes constantly search your face to understand your unspoken fears and needs. He tries in every possible way to take on your pain and problems as his own, and, in exchange, he somehow transfers some of his strength to you. It helped, it really did. The children and I decided that since John's body had been cremated, we would have a memorial service.

We thought the sooner the better; it would be easier on us all that way. I suggested the next day. The minister thought that was, perhaps, a little too soon, not allowing enough time to notify people. But I knew that wouldn't be a problem, that news of this kind of death would spread fast and that, besides, everyone who really needed to be told had already been notified. I pleaded for the early funeral.

"We need to start putting this tragedy behind us. It's going to be difficult for everyone as it is—we just can't drag out the days before the service. I don't think I can face it." I started to cry. I was overwhelmed by it all—the grief, the guilt, the suffering of my children, what others would be thinking and saying. I felt so weak, so powerless. There wasn't anything I could do to bring John back, and somehow I sensed that I had to go ahead quickly if I was to hold onto my emotional stability. I didn't have the strength to go on pleading my case. I just wanted the minister to understand and accept my request. He did understand, and he agreed that the funeral should be the next day at four in the afternoon.

There would be no music. We didn't feel this was a joyous occasion, even though the church teaches that death is not something to cry about and should be greeted with song. We didn't feel that way about this death, not a self-inflicted one. However, we did want a communion service. We even picked a passage to be read from the Bible, the Twenty-third Psalm: "Yea, though I walk through the valley of the shadow of death, I will fear no evil, for thou art with me." Perhaps we hoped that when John had walked through the valley of the shadow of death, God had been with him in some way. At least it is comforting to think so.

When all the arrangements had been agreed on, the girls went to the kitchen to help get some lunch, and Jody, quiet but less somber, went back outside with his cousin, who shared his interest in motorcycles. They both not only rode but raced. At first I hadn't been entirely happy about my son racing and riding motorcycles. It was so dangerous, and I'd seen other children badly hurt. But on that day the loud, guttural whine of the engine starting up was a reassuring sound to my ears—much better than the silence of a brooding, grief-stricken teenager. When the children had left I looked into the warm and understanding face of the minister, who sat in front of me, and asked him, "Do you believe God ever puts one human being on this earth solely for the purpose of being with another to give someone else a reason for living?"

"No," he answered without a moment's hesitation.

Perhaps he knew that was what I wanted to hear, but I prefer to believe he really meant that strong emphatic "No." Poets, songwriters, and lovers are constantly telling us that for every man there is just one woman, that we were *made* for each other, that God created "you for me." I had heard it over and over again from my husband, from the time we had first met and fallen in love when I was fourteen, until his death. He said he was nothing until I came into his life and would be nothing if I left. Never mind the other women in between; they didn't count, didn't really mean anything. I was his one true love, the woman God had intended to be his. Was it possible I *had been* meant for him to give him a reason for living?

It was reassuring to hear a man of God say no, even though I wasn't ready to believe him at that point. I felt much too responsible for my husband's death. But I was glad I had asked and glad there was no hesitation in his answer.

It was late afternoon before we drove back up the familiar dirt driveway to our house. As Taylor's car turned the corner at the top of the drive, the first thing I saw was John's sports car. Tears sprang into my eyes and spilled down my cheeks. I wiped them away, hoping the children hadn't noticed, not wanting to trigger the same reaction in them. I wanted us to walk back into the house strong, together, determined to face this and all else that lay ahead in the months and years to come. I would be mother and father—nurturer, provider, and protector. We would make it. We must make it. After all, what choice had we at that point?

As we pulled into the parking space in front of the house I looked up at the bedroom window, the one on the left. It had been broken, there had been a hole in the glass where the bullet had gone through. The hole wasn't there now. For a second I allowed myself to think that perhaps none of this had happened, John hadn't shot himself—it had all been a horrible nightmare. I looked at John's brother. "You fixed the window, didn't you?" He nodded. "Thank you," I said, and the children and I walked inside to begin facing things not so easily fixed.

Inside the house we didn't speak, we each went our separate ways—each having to face the return home alone as well as together.

I made myself walk up the stairs into the second-floor hallway. I walked past the open bedroom door, barely glancing in as I headed for the bathroom. A chill went through my body. I turned on the heat; I felt so cold. Winter must be coming early this year, I thought. I looked out of the bathroom window. The bare branches of the maple trees silhouetted against the gray November sky told me I wasn't wrong and that we'd better start getting wood in for the fireplaces. Jody would have to help more this winter, more than ever before. As I was looking out of the window I saw that the door to the motorcycle shed was open. Jody must have gone out there to work on his motorcycle. Good. He would go on racing. I didn't want that to change. I didn't want anything to change for the children because of their father's death. Even though racing had been something he primarily shared with his father, I would see to it that his racing continued. "I promise you that, Jody," I whispered as if he could hear me. "I promise you, no matter what, you will be able to go on with your moto-cross." More tears.

Then I walked out of the bathroom, just as I had done less than twenty-four hours before, out into the hall, a few steps, and I was once again standing in the doorway of my bedroom. The bed had been stripped by my brother-in-law, but the mattress was blood-stained. I would get a new one. I made myself walk into the room. I even sat on the edge of the bed. I would be sleeping here again—I shivered as another chill went through me—but not tonight. I got up, walked out of the room, and went downstairs, out the back door, and headed for the motorcycle shed.

Now the cold November air felt good, smelled clean, unrestricting.

I walked through the gate in the white board fence that divides the lawn and house from the barn and barnyard. The motorcycle shed attached to the barn had once been a stable for the children's pony. But they now had this new mode of transportation and recreation, moto-cross bikes—a whole stable of them. We all had bikes, even I. We joked that they were much better than horses because you fed motorcycles only when you rode them and you never had to clean out the stall the way we did when there was a pony living there. We all rode, but only Jody raced. He was very good and at fourteen he held promise of being exceptional, maybe even one of this country's top moto-cross riders some day.

I stopped in the open doorway of the shed, tears once again beginning to fill my eyes, blurring my vision of my son before me. He was kneeling beside the motorcycle with a wrench in his hand putting the back tire on the bike. But it wasn't his motorcycle. It was his father's, the one John had been rebuilding. Jody was going to finish the job.

"Hi," was all I could manage to say.

"Hi," he answered.

"You need a hand with anything?" I offered, wanting to be part of his bravery and desire to go on, to complete what his father had started.

"Yeah, could you hold this tire in place?"

"I sure can."

In Jody's face I saw the same determination that I was feeling—the strong will to go on, to make our lives worthwhile in spite of John's death. He didn't speak about John and neither did I. There wasn't even a feeling of his presence. His suicide would not come between my son and me. That's what I believed then. There was no resentment coming from Jody, only a feeling that *we* could and would go on. It was the beginning of many hours my son and I would spend together bending over a motorcycle or pushing one or transporting one from race to race. I would never become a motorcycle mechanic, as his father had been. But I sure could assist, and I sure wanted to.

When I'd finished helping Jody I went next door to see my mother and father. They had been away, down on the eastern shore of Maryland, when John had shot himself. We'd gotten word to them by the State Police.

They couldn't believe he had done it. We hugged one another. They asked no questions and I didn't volunteer any information that might have helped them understand. As always I knew that their love and support were there, and they knew I knew how they felt.

That night the children and I went to the home of John's mother and stepfather. Friends and relatives were coming to pay their respects. I had felt sure everyone would be looking at me in an accusing way, but that wasn't the case. John's family and friends were all sympathetic and mostly concerned about me and the children.

The evening was difficult for the children to handle or understand because the mood was light, not depressing. It was more like a party, like an Irish wake, than a gathering to mourn the death of their father. They had never had anyone close die before, so they had never experienced a strange contradiction like this. They felt sad, but everyone else around them was drinking and eating and even laughing, remembering old times and reminiscing about John. John had always said, "I want people to dance on my grave." I suppose he knew how his family would handle his death, no matter how it came about. It was the Irish way, but it was very confusing for the kids, and they said so on the way home. Marjorie said it made her sick to see how little people cared about her father's dying. I tried to explain that they cared but that they didn't show it with tears. It was not their way to let the sadness show, to publicly display their grief. She said it still gave her chills to go to a party when her father had just died.

I had to agree with her and thought to myself that it was probably that upbringing—the constant restriction of one's true feelings, the pretense of being fine when that was far from the truth—that had put John in such an emotional bind to begin with. And he had imposed that same training on Jody.

I didn't stop in my thoughts long enough to wonder just what real harm might have been done to my son by that kind of emotional restraint. Nor did I consciously think about how I might begin undoing the damage. Once again I thought things would take care of themselves. After all, John would no longer be around, and I figured my love for Jody would automatically overcome any lingering ill effects. I didn't face the possibility that Jody might suffer serious emotional problems. And I didn't talk about my thoughts to the children, when talking could have helped them all. I didn't want them to think I was finding fault with their dead father or his family.

When we got home that night the children and I decided that we would all sleep together, downstairs in the den. None of us wanted to be in our own rooms alone. Jody brought in some wood and we built a fire. It was warm, even cozy. As the four of us sat huddled together before the glow of the burning logs I felt reassured by the closeness of my kids. The phone rang. Marjorie answered it. "Hello, yes." She held the phone away from her mouth, covering it with her hand. She looked at me with an expression that wasn't judgmental, but merely questioning whether this was someone I wanted to talk to right then or whether she should make an excuse for me.

"It's Jack," she said quietly, gently. I got up, saying, "I'll take it in the kitchen." I was uncomfortable about talking to Jack in front of the children at that moment. I was uncomfortable about talking to him at all right then. I'd thought of him only briefly in the past twenty-four hours, and those thoughts had added to my pain. He had become one of my "if I hadn't" thoughts. If I hadn't fallen in love with him, I might not have been so undaunted in my effort to end things between John and me once and for all. If he hadn't told me to be firm and that I had a right to my own life, I might have been more sympathetic toward John and less concerned about my own happiness.

If I hadn't told John about Jack, he might not have felt so hopeless. If I had waited a while, until John was emotionally more stable, to tell him about Jack, my children's father might still be alive and they wouldn't be suffering his loss. Guilt had buried my feelings of love. Perhaps I was punishing myself, but I felt only resentment toward Jack when I picked up the phone. "I've got it, Marjorie." She hung up the receiver in the den.

"Why didn't you call me? I've been half crazy trying to get in touch with you." Jack was nearly hysterical. His words came fast and panicky into my ear. Jack hadn't found out about John's suicide until late that afternoon. The news director had called the news staff together and explained that I wouldn't be in to work for a while because my former husband had committed suicide. The news director didn't know Jack and I were dating, so it hadn't occurred to him to take Jack aside and tell him privately. Jack said that he had almost gotten sick on the spot. Our friend and colleague Andy Barth was so worried about Jack that he had insisted Jack go home with him. Jack was calling from the Barth's house.

"Are you all right? How about the children?" he raced on. "Where have you been? I've been so worried about you." Tears took over and doused the rapid fire of words.

"I'm all right," I said as I began coldly to answer his questions. I told him where we'd been and that we had just gotten home.

"Why didn't you call me?" he repeated.

"I didn't want to talk to you, Jack," I said with some anger.

"Why not?" he asked, pleading for a reason.

"I feel so guilty," I explained. "If it weren't for us John would be alive."

"Susan, we didn't do anything. You don't think we're the only reason John killed himself, do you?"

"I don't know; I don't know what to think. I just know last night I might have saved him; tonight he's dead."

"When am I going to see you?" he asked.

"I don't want to see you now, I can't."

"Don't you think this is exactly what John wanted?" Jack questioned, trying to get me to think rationally. "Don't you think he figured that if he killed himself you would never go on seeing me?" he continued. "Don't you understand he intended you to react this way? He couldn't have you, but I wouldn't either. He'd see to that by killing himself. Are you going to let him have his way even after death?"

"I don't know," I said with pain and frustration. "I just don't know. All I know is that the children come first now."

"Of course they do," Jack agreed. "But don't shut me out entirely," he begged.

Jack asked what my plans were and when I thought I might be coming back to work. I told him I didn't know— that first I needed to get through the funeral. I also told him that I had decided to take Jody and some of his motor-cycle friends to Jacksonville, Florida, for a National Youth Moto-Cross that was coming up in a couple of weeks.

It was a trip John had planned, but I would now carry out those plans. It was my first step in trying to show the kids that nothing would change because their father was dead. The girls were going to go with us. It would be fun; life would, must, go on.

"I wish you would see me before you go," Jack was saying. "I'm going to miss you. I'd just like to talk to you face-to-face for a few minutes."

All of a sudden I started to panic. For almost twenty years I had felt pressure from a man who had just killed himself, and now I thought I was hearing something very similar from another man. Good God, I thought, I can't face this now.

"I just want to be with my children"—I raised my voice as I spoke. "Please leave me alone." I hung up the phone without even saying goodbye and rushed back into the den, to the security of the fireside and the three young people who needed me as much as I needed them. I knew we couldn't stay locked away from the world in this one little room forever. But for tonight I felt safe here, and I desperately needed to feel that way, if only for a little while. I would take each night and each day as it came. To face everything at once was more than I had the strength to do.

The kids didn't ask what Jack had wanted or what I had said to him. And unfortunately I didn't tell them.

I missed so many opportunities for us to understand one another, simply by not talking, by not sharing thoughts, conversations, experiences—negative as well as positive.

But being physically close that night was good. We all slept soundly. The sleep relieved the exhaustion caused by the events of the past day and armed us for the strain of the day ahead.

The gray stone steeple of old St. John's church rose in the distance, above the tree line, standing out against the white sky on this cold, dismal, lifeless day. It looked as though it might rain, and it felt like snow.

Marjorie, O'Donnell, Jody, and I sat in the back of the black limousine as the driver guided the rented car through the picturesque Maryland countryside that was so familiar but glided past unnoticed that day.

Big estates on either side of the road—horse farms, mostly—hobbies and tax shelters for the wealthy gentry of the Worthington Valley, farms owned by such prominent families as Vanderbilts and Brewsters.

Marjorie had been upset because we had to ride to the church in a rented limousine—"a funeral car," as she called it. "Your uncle ordered it," I told her, "and we'll use it. No sense making waves over something like that—not now, not today."

We rounded the final bend in the winding road that put us in front of the lovely old church, a church that would look as much at home in the English countryside as here in America—a small gray stone rectangle with a prominent steeple and beautiful stained-glass windows. A three-foot high wall of the same stone surrounds the church and the old graveyard that sits to its right, which I always found more reassuring and comforting than frightening. To die in the old days was not to be abandoned, to be put in an impersonal cemetery somewhere far enough away to be forgotten, as most deceased are today. The dead were kept close to the church or the home and therefore close to the family and community, and if there was any question about your heritage, the gravestones provided as good a record as any. That way everyone had a place in life *and in death.*

Perhaps if we were all taught to believe that our life—and our death—are important, and will have a bearing on others, there might be fewer suicides.

But on this day it was hard to see those gravestones at St. John's because of all the people standing outside the church—the overflow of those who had filled every pew inside. Even the vestibule was crowded with people who would stand there throughout the service. And those outside did not leave. They would stand out in the cold until the service was over. Marjorie looked out of the window of the limousine, the funeral car. There were tears in her eyes and a note of despair in her voice, because what she saw couldn't change anything, couldn't bring her father back to life.

"Look at all the people, Mom. If Dad had only known. If Dad had only known how many people cared about him."

If he had known, I wondered to myself, would it have made a difference? Would John have been emotionally touched by this display of caring or embarrassed by it?

Are there people who would rather die than admit they need help to handle life? Even if he had known, could he have turned to any of them—could he have done it?

As we walked into the church, past all those familiar faces, I kept seeing the same expression—a sad stare of disbelief, with "Why?" written in the fold of every brow, in the questioning of puzzled eyes. The eyes searched my face for an answer, then were lowered when they saw none—no reasons, only pain.

The memorial service was as we wanted it, and it seemed right, appropriate, dignified. John would have approved. I was still concerned about pleasing him.

Marjorie sobbed openly throughout the service. O'Donnell, who, in the months to come, would face and accept the difficult but emotionally stabilizing acknowledgment that she wasn't really sorry her father was dead, because he hadn't been very nice to her when he was alive, shed very few tears. And Jody did not cry at all. Whether he was suppressing his sadness and being the "man" his father had taught him to be by not crying in public, or whether he just didn't feel quite so sad at this moment about his father's death, I never found out, but I wasn't the only one who noticed this absence of tears in the dead man's son. After the service Jody's godmother came to the limousine to console him. She leaned in at the open door, put her arms around this shy teenager, and told him how much better he would feel if he let himself cry. He never did— at least not for a long time, not until it was too late to do any good.

After the funeral, life returned to normal pretty quickly, at least outwardly. I think we all wanted it that way. O'Donnell and Jody went back to school the next week without any evidence of emotional trauma over their father's death. Teachers and students in both schools had been very supportive and sympathetic. The children had received letters expressing condolences in kind words of sympathy and friendship. I had also gotten letters from both headmasters filled with understanding and promises to keep a careful eye on my children in the months to come.

I think Jody and O'Donnell were convinced that they wouldn't experience any additional grief from insensitive kids at school making cruel remarks about their father's killing himself. And they never told me of that happening.

Marjorie had taken a year off between high school and college, so she was home, which was nice for us all. She was preparing to make her debut into Baltimore society in a couple of weeks. It was not something she wanted to do, but her father and his family had wanted it very much. So she had decided she would now go through with it because it would have pleased her Dad. She could have used the excuse that her father's recent death made it inappropriate for her to go on with those festive plans. But Marjorie reacted in the opposite way, with determination to honor her father's memory by doing something he wanted.

We were also making plans to go to Florida for that National Youth Moto-Cross. Jody, several of his friends, the girls, and I were all going. The man who owned the motorcycle shop where we bought bikes and equipment, Jack Lauterbach, was going with us. He was the grandfather of one of Jody's friends and he had been very close to John. He and John had planned the trip together for the boys. Jack was going to drive John's Winnebago motor home, and I was going to take a car. The event was coming up the last weekend in November just ten days after John's death.

I had decided not to go back to work until after that

trip. I couldn't stay away from the job too long because I needed the money. I knew my folks would give me anything I asked for—they always had—but I didn't want to lean on them too hard financially. I felt better if I was paying my own way. I wouldn't get any widow's benefits from Social Security, because John and I were divorced. But I would get some money for support of the children, and that would help with their education.

Jack Bowden had not called since the night before the funeral, and I had not called him. I think he had wisely decided to give me some time and space in which to sort out my thoughts and begin to try and deal with the feelings of guilt. It was in Jacksonville that those feelings came to a head.

After several hectic days at the racetrack I went off by myself one night to be alone with my thoughts, and everything came crashing in on me. I was walking on the Jacksonville beach, watching the moon shimmer on the dark, unsettled ocean. The lights from the hotel dotted the darkness, reminding me that the kids were in there, probably having pillow fights or riding up and down in the elevator, driving the other guests crazy. Let them have their fun while I have a few minutes to myself, I thought. I was physically exhausted from running back and forth across the moto-cross course, and I was beginning to realize how emotionally drained I was from all that had happened since John's death.

I had been trying very hard to be strong, to set an example that the children could follow. If I was up and going about the business of living, then maybe they would also. But now I felt terribly depressed, alone, and angry. What was I doing on this beach, by myself, hundreds of miles from my home and my job? I began talking out loud to the dead man who had put me in this position, who had left me alone to carry on. "I don't belong here, John. *You* should be here. *You* planned this trip. *You* wanted to bring Jody to Jacksonville. *You* wanted him to race in a national competition. *You* should have seen this through. Why didn't you have the courage to face your problems? Why weren't the children enough for you to live for? *You* would have really enjoyed this trip."

Tears of anger and frustration poured out as the surf pounded beside me. I felt dizzy and weak. My legs buckled, and I fell to my knees. The anger was again giving way to guilt, and I began talking to myself. "John would be here if it weren't for you. You're selfish, self-centered, and uncaring. You pushed him to the edge and then sat quietly in that bathroom as he went over it. Don't feel sorry for yourself and angry at John. You made this all happen; now you live with it." I was far away from what little security I knew—the family farm in Maryland and the world where I really felt like somebody, where I was special, where I had made a name for myself, the world of television. I wanted to go back to that world. I wanted to go home. And I wanted to see Jack. That realization rushed to the front of my brain like the waves hitting the shore, washing away everything else for a few moments, leaving only his image. I wanted and needed to talk to my friend. I wanted to be close to my lover. I didn't want to face all these feelings and problems without him. Those thoughts brought more guilt and more tears. "How can you think about what you want at a time like this when your children need all your attention, all the help and guidance you can give them? And Jody needs to know that he will be able to go on racing, that *you* want him to race."

I felt such conflict, such grief and guilt. How would I

ever be able to cope? Where would all this end? What was going to happen to us?

I rolled over in the sand, stared up at the stars for a while, then closed my eyes. But as I felt the relief of sleep start to release me temporarily from my turmoil, I forced my eyes back open and turned my head toward the hotel where my children waited for me. I was the only one they had left, their only parent. I somehow found the strength I didn't think was there to get back up on my feet. I stood still for a moment to steady my shaky legs and to try to calm my pulse, which was throbbing in my temples. I was still dizzy and felt sick to my stomach. I took a deep breath, wiped the tears from my face, and began to walk back up the beach, back to where I belonged, where I was needed, where I wanted to be.

We would go home together but not until the racing was over. We would see that through first, then we would go home. I called Jack later that night. The tears and words of need poured out of me and into the phone. He was so glad to hear from me. There was no hint of any lingering hurt or irritation because I had hung up on him. He had understood. He was relieved that I did want to see him. We both understood that this wasn't the end of my emotional turmoil, but at least we would face it together. We agreed to meet as soon as I got home. He would come out to the house and bring his four-year-old son, Christopher. We knew we'd have to back up a bit and start over. He knew that my children were my prime concern. That isn't to say that we wouldn't have words and misunderstandings over this in the months to come, that I wouldn't feel torn between being a mother and being his lover. But at that time it was clear in both our minds where my priorities lay.

When, several weeks later, we eventually got a few minutes alone, just the two of us, our physical reunion was an intensely emotional one. As I lay in his arms I felt a flood of tears well up inside of me that spilled from my eyes onto his bare shoulder. These were tears I knew I could not control, because they came not from sadness of the past or fear of the future but from the sheer joy of the moment, from the blending of two souls into one highly sensitized being. Could there ever be any problems that we, together, could not conquer? I didn't think so, not then, at that powerful moment. But I continued to be haunted by feelings of guilt over our relationship.

It was difficult if not impossible for me to commit myself completely to someone when I felt my happiness with that person had been achieved at the expense of someone else's life. It was hard not to say, "I don't deserve this pleasure. I shouldn't feel good." As a self-imposed judge and jury, I punished myself by removing the cause of the happiness. Then I would feel bad, which is the way I figured I should feel for causing someone to commit suicide, and I had also made the other person, the accomplice in the crime, suffer as well. After all, he too deserved to be punished. Even if I had been aware of the psychological process, it would have been hard not to give in to it.

Looking back, I realize that I could have used some professional guidance. We all could have. But I never thought about it. Not my family or friends or even the schools, no one at work even casually asked if the children or I were getting any help to handle John's suicide.

I now know that it's very important for all members of a family in which a suicide occurs to get counseling in order to be able to deal with the suicide and the individual feelings resulting from it. Good counseling right away can also be useful in heading off emotional trouble that may occur later on. Both Marjorie and O'Donnell eventually sought counseling on their own, and I think they both benefited from it.

The one who needed it most relied completely on my guidance, and it never dawned on me that he might need therapy. Nor did I know that he might be a prime candidate for suicide simply because his father had died that way. Jody really seemed fine to me. He seemed to be adjusting well. He wasn't depressed. His friends were coming to the house. They joked and kidded and horsed around like any other teenage boys. Jody was doing well in school. In fact, his homeroom teacher and the headmaster had both sent notes home saying that Jody had apparently handled his father's suicide well, that he had apparently made a good adjustment. I wasn't worried. I saw a happy youngster who seemed to be enjoying life. I even remember wishing I was doing as well. Jody had taken on a new independence. He was the man of the house. He seemed comfortable in this role.

Jody even liked Jack. They weren't close yet, but I thought that would come. They really hadn't had a chance to get to know each other at that point. I knew that Jody thought Jack was a bit too citified. He knew Jack would never be interested in motorcycles or many other things he liked, but he didn't seem to resent him. But then I never asked Jody what he thought of Jack, so how do I really know?

The sadness of what I didn't ask and therefore didn't know overwhelms me at times, making it hard to go on as I pursue my search for the truth about the desperate way my son ended his life.

CHAPTER 4
ATTEMPTED LIFE
AFTER SUICIDE
JANUARY 1975

*T*HE alarm went off. I looked over at the clock radio—6:15. I looked up at the window— mornings are so cold and dark in January, so uninviting. I looked over at the other side of the bed. The top sheet was still pulled tight, tucked in as if I hadn't moved all night. Was I afraid that in my sleep I would move, move to *that* side of the bed—where John had slept, where we had made love, where we had conceived our children, where he lay when he shot himself? I quickly rolled over and put my feet on the cold floor—on my side of the bed— and stood up to face another day.

I wonder where Marjorie is right now? I thought to my-self. It's already the end of this day in Africa. Please, dear God, make her all right. Marjorie and a girl friend had been planning the trip to Africa since their graduation from high school last June. Marjorie was concerned about going ahead with those plans so soon after her father's death, but I argued that she should go on with her life just as she had planned. Her father would have wanted it that way, and I certainly did.

I didn't want any of the children to have their lives completely turned around because their father had committed suicide. I didn't want that to cripple their growth and independence. I didn't want Marjorie, who was almost nineteen and ready to begin experiencing life on her own, to think she now had to huddle close to home to take care of me. I knew that I would be worried and anxious about her safety the entire time she was in Africa, but I would handle that so she wouldn't have to deal with the emotional and mental suffocation that restrictions on her independence might have caused then. As much as it hurt, and it did hurt, I had to let her go. Besides, perhaps she needed to get away to gain some perspective on what she had just been through.

Several times Marjorie had told me of the guilt she felt about not being home on the night her father shot himself. She believed that she might have stopped him. "If I had been here he wouldn't have done it," she had said. That particular "if I had" plagued her more than any other. She had to deal with those feelings—face them and then discard them or learn to live with them. I knew in my heart that she wouldn't be able to escape those thoughts right away, not by going to Africa—or to anywhere else on earth. But if there was a chance that she could, I wanted her to take it.

When we were in Jacksonville for the moto-cross I realized that I needed familiar surroundings and my family in order to cope. I realized I needed to stay close to home to deal with John's death. But I couldn't impose my wishes on my daughter. I couldn't order her to sit safely within my reach for my benefit.

I'm not sure now that that philosophy is a good one. I'm not sure it isn't better to let family and friends know of your needs, especially if those needs mean giving on their part—giving of their time, their love, their physical and emotional strength, their presence. When you rely on people and they know you are relying on them, they feel necessary, important, needed. It is only through giving and personal commitment that love grows. It is only when you sacrifice for people you care about that you begin to realize the full potential of the love that you feel for them. If you are led to believe by someone you love, who apparently loves you, that his or her life will progress and grow and be fulfilling even if you are not around—if, in other words, you are not really needed to improve the quality of that person's life—you are bound to ask, "What's so important about this feeling between us? What is there about this relationship that's special? What's important about me in that person's life?" The answer usually arrived at is "nothing," and feelings fade or drift, unnourished, in a stagnant state for months or even years.

I hope Marjorie knows how much I love her, I thought. I hope she's all right. I'll be so glad when she comes home and I can tell her, show her. Please, dear God, make her all right.

I walked across the bedroom out into the hall, reaching up to switch on the hall light and the one at the top of the landing to Jody's room. I followed the light up the stairs, stopping halfway to the third floor where, as usual, I called out to wake up my son, "Jody, are you awake? It's time to get up."

"Okay, Mom"—a sleepy voice, trying very hard to sound awake, came back to me.

I smiled. He always made me smile even when he didn't

intend to. I walked back down the stairs, turned right, down two more steps, and opened the door to O'Donnell's room.

"Okay, another day, time to get up. School's awaiting."

"Aw—no, not yet," came in a muffled voice from under the covers.

"Yes, yes, come on. I think you still need to iron a uniform, the one you didn't iron last night."

"It doesn't have to be ironed. I can wear it the way it is."

"No, you can't, come on—up with you."

Marjorie was in Africa, but for O'Donnell, Jody, and me getting back to the business of living meant returning to the daily routine and facing the familiar (friends, schoolmates, coworkers, and, in my case, the public at large) with a very unfamiliar thing—suicide.

The television viewers knew I had been off the air because of my former husband's death (there was a death notice in the paper, just his name and "died suddenly"), but most did not know the circumstances surrounding his death. Because of that, there was the ordeal of explaining that John had taken his own life each time someone said, "I heard about your husband's death—my God, what happened, he was so young!" There would be a few uncomfortable stammers from me as I pulled my thoughts and emotions together and tried to push aside my embarrassment and the embarrassment I knew the questioner would feel as soon as I had answered.

"Suicide."

I always said it as softly as possible to try to ease the shock, but there is no gentle way to say someone has killed himself. The word and its meaning are harsh, destructive, and accusing, and always provoke another question.

"Good God, Susan, *why?*"

"Personal problems between us. He wanted a reconciliation and I couldn't give it to him."

"Oh, my God, how awful . . . I mean for you and the
kids . . . and for him, of course."

Their eyes would drop to avoid mine. What could they
possibly say?

I'd try to ease the tension and reduce the embarrassment
they were feeling.

"The children and I are doing okay. It's a terrible tragedy, but I think we'll be all right. I hope."

It was always awkward, and perhaps that's why most of
those who knew how my husband had died didn't say
anything to me. They just avoided the subject of John's
death altogether.

*We've never been told what to say to someone who has
had a suicide in the family. What I needed to hear was the
same thing that might be said to anyone else who has experienced the death of someone close—"I'm truly sorry
for your pain, and is there anything I can do? If you need
to talk about it, I'm a good listener. I've got a comfortable
shoulder to cry on." And I needed to know that it was
really meant. Everyone believes no one wants to talk about
suicide, that it's best left undiscussed, that if you don't
talk about it, it will be forgotten and will go away. Nothing could be further from the truth.*

*Survivors of suicide, as we are now called, need to talk
about what they have experienced and are feeling. I feel
strongly about that because I made the same kind of mistake with my children. I never encouraged them to talk
about their thoughts or feelings concerning the death of
their father and the way it happened, and I never spoke to
them about my thoughts—the guilt, the pain, the night-
mares, the recurring image of their father lying on the bed*

with a gun in his hand, bleeding from the head. I couldn't bring myself to open up to the three people who mattered most in my life. I didn't want them to know I had come to hate John for doing this to us, and I didn't want them to hate their father on my behalf.

I thought if I didn't talk about their father's suicide and about his frailties and faults and talked only about his good points and achievements—and there were many—then the kids would rid themselves of any feelings of disappointment in their father. That they would remember him only in a good way, and not feel a sense of shame when his name was mentioned. But what I failed to do in this approach was to give them a realistic, balanced look at their father and what he had done. Never did I show them my anger at John for what he had done. Never did I say what a stupid, selfish act suicide is—that it caused us all great pain and accomplished nothing but the loss of a life. I was too afraid that if I criticized their father, my children would retaliate by saying his death was my fault, that they would turn away from me.

But even if they had, it would have been worth it, because such feelings, if they existed, needed to be vented. I should have trusted my children and the strength of our love for each other. By glorifying the memory of John I made him and what he had done bigger than life. It was a great mistake and a devastating disservice to my children.

Breakfast was fixed, but I didn't feel like packing lunches that day. I turned around as Jody walked through the kitchen door.

"Do you mind buying your lunch today?"

"Uh-uh," he said, shaking his head. "I don't care. They

have spaghetti today—that's better than peanut butter sandwiches."

"Good, I'll give you the money that I have for your racing this weekend and you can use it for lunch instead."

"No way," Jody protested.

"I'm just kidding—you know better than that. I guess we can still afford a school lunch and the races."

"Can Eddie go with us Sunday? His bike is ready to race, but he doesn't have any way to get there."

"Of course. How about Dean?"

"His grandfather's going to take him."

"Good. What about Ricky?"

"I don't know. I'll ask him today."

"He's always welcome to go with us. He can come out and spend the weekend. You can go to his house after school, and I'll pick up both of you there after work. Call him at home right now and ask him—he hasn't left for school yet."

"You call—his stepmother or father will probably answer and they won't like me bothering them in the morning."

"Jody, they won't mind you calling, you won't be bothering them. If they answer, just ask to speak to Ricky."

"Yes, they will—you call."

"Jody, people can't bite your head off over the phone. You just pick it up and dial the number like this."

I couldn't believe how shy Jody was about talking to people, even over the phone. He had always been that way. But it had gotten worse as he entered adolescence. I was never like that as a teenager. In fact, I was just the opposite—self-assured, outgoing, able to talk to adults and boys with the same ease as when talking to my best girl friends. And Marjorie and O'Donnell didn't seem to suffer such shyness. Maybe Jody got it from his father or maybe it's a teenage trait that boys have more trouble with than girls. Or maybe I just protected him too much. Maybe I should have forced him to make calls like that one. I know I should have!

"Hello, Marcie. Hi, this is Susan White. We thought it would be great if Ricky could come out for the weekend and go to the races with Jody on Sunday."

Jody listened as I tried to arrange the weekend for him. After a few minutes I said goodbye and hung up.

"What did she say?" Jody asked.

"She said Ricky has to stay home this weekend and work around the house with his father."

I looked up at the kitchen clock.

"We've got to get going or you'll be late for school."

"I'm ready," he said.

"Well, I'm not. If you had made that phone call, I would be dressed by now."

"Ma-uh-um?" he said, drawing out the word "Mom" and putting a question mark at the end. "You couldn't even get the curlers out of your hair that fast, much less get dressed—and don't forget all that makeup."

"Very funny. I'll be beautiful before you finish your breakfast—and *eat* an English muffin. Cereal isn't enough to power that gigantic brain of yours."

I bounded up the stairs two at a time, stopping in O'Donnell's room to check her progress. She was in the bathroom between her room and Marjorie's, fixing her hair.

"What are your plans for tonight?" I asked.

"I'd like to stay at school for play rehearsal and then spend the night in the upper-school dorm with Frannie."

The private girls' school O'Donnell attended had some day students and some boarders. She had talked often about wanting to stay at school herself, even though we lived less than a half hour away from the school. The companionship of friends, teachers, and houseparents at the school provided a more stable family, a more comfortable atmosphere for my younger daughter than her father and I had been able to do. It was sad, but it was true.

"I was hoping you were going to be home tonight with Jody, because Lowell James—you know, the eleven o'clock co-anchor—is leaving Channel 2 and going to a station in Detroit, and there's going to be a farewell party for him tonight. Jack and I want to stop by for a little while. I guess Jody could stay here alone for an hour or two, but I need you to drive him home after school. I don't have to go to the party, but I think I should. Can you bring him home and pick up something for his dinner on the way?"

"Yeah, sure, I'll do that. What do you want me to get?"

"I don't know—a TV dinner that he can fix. Ask him what kind he wants. I've got to get dressed. Call me at work when you get home, okay?"

"Okay."

I went into my room, pulled out a suit and blouse, looked at the blouse, put it back in the closet and pulled out a dressier one. If I was going to the party I needed something a little fancier than a tailored shirt. I dressed quickly, took out the curlers, and sat down at my dressing table to comb my hair and put on some makeup. I could complete the job after I got to the station. Jody walked into the room and sat on the edge of the bed to watch me as I went through my daily beauty routine. He did this almost every morning as he waited for me to get ready to drive him to school. Sometimes I would talk, sometimes he would do the talking, sometimes neither of us spoke. It was a time we shared that didn't need forced conversation to make it okay.

I hesitated before speaking today because I didn't feel comfortable about what I was going to say. I was worried about Jody's reaction when I told him I was going out that night and leaving him alone. I hadn't done that since John's death. The past couple of months Jack had been coming out to the house for dinner or just to hang around the farm on a Saturday or Sunday. Jack even joined an occasional Monopoly game with Jody and his friends. Sometimes it was just Jody and Jack. Jody liked those times. I could tell. He liked the attention and he liked Jack's making the effort to spend an hour or so with him. Those were my favorite times too. I'd be in the kitchen fixing dinner and I'd hear them laughing and talking in the den. That made me feel really good. It was a tonic that freed me of tension. Since John's death, the few times Jack and I had been alone, at his apartment or out for an evening of dinner and the movies, were times when Jody was staying at a friend's house and O'Donnell was at school.

Jody would be fifteen in March and he certainly was capable of staying by himself for a few hours—he had done it many times before . . . before his father's death. But I felt funny about leaving him in the house alone now, so soon after the loss of his dad. I was afraid he would think I didn't care about him, that he would think I preferred to be with Jack, that he would resent me for wanting to spend time alone with Jack, especially if it meant he had to be alone. I'm not sure why I thought it was important to go to that party. Maybe I was beginning to feel the need

to socialize more. Maybe Jody had apparently adjusted so
well after his father's death that I didn't think it would
really be a problem. Most likely it was that blind optimism
of mine that everything would be all right no matter what
I did.

*Looking back, I realize my going was completely un-
necessary and insensitive to Jody. How could I leave him
alone and go to a party? I wouldn't have wanted to have
been left alone if our roles had been reversed. But I never
thought this kind of thing through. I simply did things. I
reacted without reflecting. God knows, it wasn't because I
didn't love my son.*

"Jody." I spoke softly with gentleness in my voice.
"Jody, there's going to be a party tonight for Lowell
James, who's leaving Channel 2. Jack and I are going to
stop by after work for a little while. We won't be long,
but it means you're going to have to stay here alone for an
hour or two tonight."

"What about O'Donnell?" he protested.

"She'll drive you home and pick up a TV dinner for you
on the way, whatever kind you want," I said, knowing as I
spoke that it was not the kind of bribe that would pacify
him on this occasion.

"What's she going to do after she brings me home?"

"She has to go back to school for play rehearsal, and
then she's going to spend the night at school."

"It's not fair. Why do I have to stay here? When I get
my license I'm going to go out every night."

"No, you're not—don't be silly. I won't be late, I
promise."

"You were going to pick up me and Ricky, and now
you won't be home at all—how come?"

"I *will be home,* Jody. I was going to bring you and Ricky home and then drive back in town to the party. But since Ricky can't come, I asked O'Donnell to drive you home to save me a trip."

I took my eyes away from my reflection in the makeup mirror and looked at my son. He was hurt; the selfish words asking "what about me?" were a cover. I had chosen to be with someone else and leave him alone. I was ready to cancel all the plans and just come home after work and be with him. But I knew this day would have to come sooner or later; perhaps sooner would be easier than later. *I wanted Jody to grow and mature without relying too heavily on me as a companion. I loved him and loved being with him, but I didn't want him to become too dependent on our relationship. What I didn't realize at the time was that Jody needed to feel secure. He needed to be sure of my love, my dependability. He needed to know that I would always be there. His father had left him; he needed to know that his mother would never do that. He had to be sure of me and the fact that he was more important to me than anyone or anything outside the family.*

Jody got up from the bed and walked out of the room and down the steps. It was a slow, deliberate descent, with each foot dropping solidly onto the step below, sending back the message of his mood—rejection—a pensive pout not suffered entirely in silence.

Guilt gnawed at my insides like the hunger of a starving person. A wave of nausea actually swept through me. Had I failed my son by putting my interests before his wants, his needs? I looked at the clock. I didn't have time then to tackle the problem or cope with depressing feelings, so I dismissed them. I pushed the problem aside, as I always did when I didn't have a handy solution, always believing everything would work out for the best. It's not that big a deal, I rationalized—a couple of hours alone. I gathered up my makeup and hair spray, shoved them into my purse, and took off down the stairs, calling back in the direction of O'Donnell's room as I went, "Don't forget to call me when you get home, O'Donnell."

"I will, Mom—call you, that is, not forget."

"Have a good day. Good luck with the play practice."

"Okay, bye."

"And drive carefully."

"I will."

O'Donnell was now using the car John had bought Marjorie for graduation, and Marjorie intended to drive John's car when she got back from Africa. Three drivers in the family and three cars. Not good, I had thought. It makes us less reliant on one another. So why allow it? A necessary convenience, I had convinced myself, for those living in the country so far from school and work. I grabbed my heavy wool cape out of the hall closet and threw it around my shoulders.

Jody was already outside, sitting in the cold car waiting for me. More suffering on his part, more guilt on mine. I jumped in beside him, put the key in the ignition, and started the engine of my Ford Torino.

"Boy, it's cold today. You should have worn your heavy ski sweater."

"Uh-uh, this is okay."

"Ooh-kay, here we go, off and running in a cloud of dust—or maybe frost would be more like it."

My answer to everything was to be cheery, and problems would go away. They used to call me Susie Sunshine at the

*station. I'd have a smile and an encouraging word for prac-
tically every occasion. Laughter may be good medicine,
but a constant smile can actually be injurious if it replaces
serious reflection on problems that need addressing.*

I turned on the radio as we drove down the driveway—
a little music and news to replace the silence during the
lulls in the conversation, which would be many that day.
I didn't mention Jody being home alone, because to bring
it up again would have meant dealing with it. That's
something I would do now, but I didn't do it then. It was
as if I thought everything unpleasant would take care of
itself by magic—go away and never come back to further
dispel the life of harmony I always convinced myself was
just around the bend.

It takes about thirty minutes to drive to the private
boys' school where Jody had been a student since the fifth
grade. We had been pretty happy with the school because
it challenged Jody's very bright mind. As an eighth-grader
he was in an advanced math section doing work on a
twelfth-grade level. In fact, he had been tested at Johns
Hopkins University in part of its program for gifted math
and science students. Jody had been offered the opportunity to enroll in the university to take math courses and
get credit for them toward his college degree. We had decided against letting him take advantage of the offer, believing it might not be good to push a shy fourteen-year-
old into a classroom situation with much older students.
Our thoughts were that a child who already had a problem
socializing might withdraw even more under those circumstances. It may have been a mistake not to let him
feel the confidence and strength of his full potential in
this area. But he was able to get the advanced math at the
school he was now attending, and he seemed to feel pretty

good about himself and his ability to excel in that field, beyond most of his peers.

The only problem that had arisen with the school came in the area of sports. Jody was a good athlete and had played on the seventh- and eighth-grade soccer team. But in the spring, when he went out for lacrosse, he was confronted with a negative attitude toward motorcycle riding that brought about the end of his participation in sports at the school. He and the other boys who showed up for the first day of lacrosse practice were told by the coach—who knew many of them rode moto-cross on weekends—that anyone who intended to ride motorcycles during lacrosse season had better forget about playing on his team. Feeling a strong need to remain loyal to his moto-cross, Jody got up and walked out of the locker room. It caused a separation between Jody and the strong sports segment of the school. And I'm afraid he lost his sense of belonging, of school spirit, because of it.

I never wanted to be a meddling mother, but that's one time I wish I had stepped in and spoken up for my child's rights. I know that the coach was concerned about putting someone on the team who might get hurt while riding a motorcycle, which would mean that he and the lacrosse team would be out a player, with all the practice and training going down the drain. But seventh or eighth grade or even high school is not the time or place to have such concerns. In professional sports which are a business, such considerations are appropriate, and perhaps even in college, but certainly not in high school. I consider sports an extension of the regular education process, a subject outside the classroom, contributing to the growth and experience of maturing children—their mental and emotional growth as well as their physical development. Taking part in sports teaches children to work with others for a common goal and to share with teammates in victory or—equally important—defeat.

We all get so caught up in winning, we forget about the importance of participation and losing. It may sound trite, but how a kid plays a game can contribute greatly to how he lives his life. Winning, being first in everything, is not the only reason or reward for playing a game or for living. There are also lessons to be learned from losing, and perhaps those lessons are better preparation for adulthood than winning could ever provide.

Sports aside, Jody *was* getting a good education, and most of his teachers seemed genuinely interested in him. I felt reassured, and I thought, especially now with the loss of his father, that an all-boys school, with mostly male teachers, was the best place for him. At least I didn't have to worry about there not being any men around to provide examples or role models for Jody. I knew he would get guidance and discipline from male authority figures, and I knew how very important that would be during the next couple of years.

Now, I thought, if I could just be the kind of *mother* he needed to see him through those difficult times. If caring was enough, we'd have no trouble. "I love this kid more than I could ever put into words. But is love enough?" I questioned myself. It had to be, especially the kind of love we shared. It was strong and special. I'd always felt we had more going for us than the average mother and son, a unique, unspoken understanding. It seemed we could look at each other and know what the other was thinking. Certain relationships might fall apart, but I felt confident ours wouldn't, not Jody's and mine—we'd always be strong. We were so comfortable with each other.

He'd chatter away, I'd listen. I'd chatter, he'd listen. But more than that, there was an indescribable something that had always existed between us—natural sympathy or compatibility, chemistry, or whatever.

I looked over at my son. He *was* growing up. The light blond hair was getting darker and longer than I liked. The cute pug nose was getting longer and wider and would soon be too big for his boyish face. The eyebrows were dark, and there was a hint of hair on his upper lip. His head turned toward me and our eyes met. I smiled and asked: "Do you know why the elephant bought designer jeans?"

"No."

"Because the elephant down the street wears them."

"Mom, that's really dumb."

"It made you smile."

He looked down at his books and didn't say anything the rest of the way to school.

I love you so much Jody, I thought to myself. So much. *I thought it, but I didn't say it—a holdover from John's telling me not to smother my son with affection. Anyway, I figured Jody knew how I felt. But did he? He needed to hear "I love you" from me. He needed to hear it and I needed to say it out loud. But I didn't.* I pulled in off the main road and merged with the traffic inching its way around the circular drive in front of the big white mansion that is now the administration building of St. Paul's School. When we got to the right of the circle Jody pulled open the door as I came to an abrupt stop, just long enough for him to bail out but not long enough to aggravate the parent in the car behind us. Teamwork, we called it when we bragged about our maneuver.

"Bye," he said matter-of-factly, without emotion, as his

feet hit the ground and his free hand reached to shove the car door closed.

"See you later, alligator," I called out just before the sound of the slamming door cut off any further communication.

Even on bad days, driving Jody to school was among my favorite times with him. I had pushed the problem away and was left with only the joy of his existence, convinced everything would solve itself. I smiled as I guided the car toward the station and prepared to face the other part of my life.

Since I went directly to work after driving Jody to school, I always got to the station about an hour before I needed to be there. Most days I had to stay until seven-thirty and the end of the evening newscast, and therefore I wasn't due until ten. Starting at nine made for a really long day, but it gave me a chance to read the paper, get some mail out of the way, and generally get a jump on the day's activities. Also, it provided a little social time—a cup of coffee and some casual conversation with those on the early shift in the newsroom. For the most part I genuinely like the people in television news and enjoy spending time with them.

Each morning I looked forward to Jack's arrival. It was so good to see him walk through the door and into the newsroom. He was usually late. His tie would be untied; he hated ties, and refused to tie them until he had to. But it isn't his nature to be sloppy. His shirt and suit would be neatly pressed and his hair perfectly combed, every hair in place. It's just one of the many things about him that I love and one of the reasons I looked forward to seeing him every morning.

My being "in love" with him also had a little something to do with my being glad to see him each day—experiencing that feeling of excitement and electricity that flows between two people newly in love. It doesn't matter if those people are over thirty-five and forty; age cannot act as a barrier to stop it. When Jack walked into the newsroom each morning I literally felt giddy and breathless, like a teenage girl being called for her first date. Our eyes would meet, we'd smile at each other, and we both knew we were glad that the other was there.

"Hi, I love you," he said as he stood before me at my desk.

"I love you too, I really do."

"Good. How are you today?"

"Pretty good," I lied.

There were many times I didn't want to break the mood of romance with my problems. That was one of them.

"We're going out tonight, right?" he asked.

"We sure are, if you call going to a farewell party 'going out.' "

"Well, it's a start. You want to come back to my place after the party for a little while?"

"I would really love to, but I can't. Jody will be home alone tonight, and he's not very happy about it and neither am I."

"Why?"

"I just don't feel right about leaving him alone so soon after his father's death."

"I understand," Jack said. "Well, I have to go to Annapolis today. Do you want to meet me at the party?"

"I think that would be best. It's really on my way home,

so we might as well have both cars with us, to save your picking me up somewhere and then having to take me back for my car."

"Okay, I'll see you there, then."

"Okay, about eight-thirty?"

"Yeah—I'm only in the six o'clock newscast tonight, so I should be able to get there by then."

I looked down at the papers on the top of my desk.

"Hey," Jack whispered, to get my attention again. "I love you very much," he said to reassure me.

"I know," I said, "and I love you. It all just seems so complicated."

"It'll be all right. You'll see."

"I hope you're right," I said, truly hoping he *was right.*

"I've got to go. I'm late now. The governor's having a press conference in forty-five minutes."

Late that afternoon, around five-thirty, I was about to call home. I had my hand on the phone when it rang.

"Hi, Mom, we're home." O'Donnell was calling as I had asked her to do.

"You got Jody and Jody's dinner, right?"

"Yeah, he said he didn't want a TV dinner, but I got one anyway."

"Why didn't he want one?"

"I don't know. He's just being obnoxious, a creepy kid."

"Let me talk to him."

"Jody," she yelled, "Mom wants to talk to you."

"Hello." He sounded sullen.

"Jody, why didn't you want a TV dinner?"

"I don't know. I just don't feel like one."

"What kind did O'Donnell get?"

"Turkey."

"Well, you like that."

"I know."

"Well, you'll probably feel like eating it later."

Silence.

"Jody, I'll tell you what, the party I'm going to is out toward Reisterstown. I'm meeting Jack there, so I'll probably have time to get some chocolate chip ice cream and bring it home before going to the party. Would you like that?"

"Okay." His voice brightened at the suggestion.

"Good. I'll see you as soon as I can, right after I get off the air. Let me talk to O'Donnell again, okay?"

"Okay. O'Donnell," he shouted, "Mom wants to talk to you again."

"Yes?" O'Donnell said as she picked up the upstairs phone.

"You're going back to school now, right?"

"Right."

"Will you be home tomorrow?"

"I'm not sure. I might stay there for the weekend."

"Well, that's all right. I'll be home with Jody. Just let me know, okay?"

"Okay."

"Bye, darling, and have a good weekend, if I don't see you."

"Okay."

I hung up the phone. Maybe if we lived closer to town life would be easier, I thought as I turned my attention back to my report and getting ready to go on the air.

By eight-thirty I'd been home to deliver the chocolate chip ice cream. I kidded around with Jody and made him laugh. He seemed okay, but he got quiet and moody when I started to leave. "I'll be home before you have time to miss me," I told him—trying hard to believe it—and rushed out before I could change my mind. I was hurrying so that I wouldn't be late meeting Jack. Although I knew he wouldn't be there on time—he was never on time—I wanted to be there when I'd said I would, just in case.

What is it about me that *must always* please the men in my life? I wondered to myself. It seemed I'd never out-grown the need for male approval, and my efforts to avoid men's disapproval had consumed much of my life. I was still seeking that special pat on the head and words of praise that I'd gotten as a child from my father—and try-ing to overcome the rejection I'd felt when he let me go at fifteen.

It wasn't until years later—very recently, as a matter of fact—that I got up the courage to ask my parents why they had *not* had my marriage annulled. I went to their home on a Sunday evening, sat down in the den with the two of them, and blurted out, "I need to know why you didn't have my marriage to John annulled."

"Oh, that's easy," my mother said. "Two reasons. Our lawyer said not to. He thought you might be pregnant. And Johnny's mother asked us not to. She thought you might help settle Johnny down."

"What would have been the use?" my father added. "You had spent the night in a hotel with him. You had had intercourse. I would have been turning a young girl loose who was worldly-wise."

They figured it was better to have a married fifteen-year-old daughter than to deal with an unmarried one who wasn't a virgin. It was the old-fashioned way. A girl who'd had sex was better off married, no matter what her age.

"And one of my friends," Daddy was continuing, "told

me not to do anything I'd be sorry for later. I might end up losing a daughter and a son-in-law."

"Oh, there were lots of comments and suggestions," my mother added. "Your godfather, Mac, wanted to tear Johnny apart, limb from limb."

Good for Mac, I thought. I always did like him. "You talked to everybody but me," I said meekly. "We never talked about this with each other, before a decision was made or afterward."

"No," said Daddy. "What would have been the use?"

"I wanted you to have it annulled. I was praying that you would save me from the mistake that I'd made."

"Then it's your fault," Daddy shot back defensively. "You should have said something. If you'd told us how you felt, we would have gladly done anything you wanted. We thought you wanted to be married to Johnny."

I looked at Daddy's face. He was hurt. Daddy became defensive only when he was hurt, when he thought he was being blamed for something he hadn't done or had had no control over. I didn't want him to think I was blaming him for my years of unhappiness or for John's suicide. I knew my parents had done what they thought was best for me at the time. I knew they would never have done anything intentionally to hurt me. In fact I knew that by allowing me to stay married at fifteen they had suffered greatly themselves. They were left with much anguish and a feeling of personal loss. Right after John and I were married, we lived with my folks, and I watched how their lives were changed and saw how deeply it affected them emotionally. For months after my marriage my mother walked around the house merely going through the motions. Often while washing the dishes, or setting the dining-room table, or making a bed, when her thoughts were elsewhere, most likely on me, and she thought she was alone I heard her sigh a heavy soulful sigh revealing deep sadness from within.

And my father, an outgoing, gregarious man, became quiet and preoccupied. His sunshine had been taken away. His dreams for his little girl had been shattered. There would be no Olympic swimming champion, which he was sure I'd be; there would be no college graduate. His personal pride and joy now belonged to someone else. It hurt him but he let it happen because he honestly thought it was what I wanted and what might eventually be best for me. And that was his primary concern. But we didn't talk about it. We didn't talk about their pain or mine.

When John committed suicide, they didn't even ask if I knew why he had done it. I guess they didn't want to put me on the spot, or make me talk about something unpleasant, or let me think that they were blaming me. Daddy just said, "If there's anything we can do, you know we're here." And my parents were always there for everything I needed except the soul-searching, revealing conversation.

"We never talked to each other about any problems," I told them. "I didn't know what to say. I didn't even know how to begin, so I didn't."

My parents were probably not much different from most others when it comes to talking to children about problems. Many of us try to prepare children for life without this vitally important ingredient. We teach our kids to walk and talk, to ride bicycles and drive cars. We spend a lot of time entertaining them and generating fun for them. We send them to school and to church, but rarely do we make a conscious effort to see that a child develops and refines the ability to face, handle, and solve problems. It might be the single most important lesson our children can learn.

Some adults whisper about problems behind closed doors so as not to "upset the kids." Others yell about them in anger. Neither approach gives a child the idea that difficulties can be rationally dealt with, talked about sensibly, and that solutions can be found.

And solving our kids' problems for them is certainly not the answer. We might be able to do that when they are little, but not when they grow up. Sheltering our young children from problems makes the onslaught of teenage problems all the more difficult to deal with—when Mom and Dad can no longer make them disappear.

I think that we can and should guide our children and help them with their troubles, but not by freeing them entirely from the responsibility and experience of successful problem solving. Ignoring problems altogether is even worse.

"You never talked about your problems," I said searchingly to my father.

"We never liked to admit we had any," he answered.

I was taken aback by my father's candor. It would have been so much better if we had discussed this years ago, I thought.

I never would have had the nerve to start such a conversation if it hadn't been for Jack. He was teaching me to communicate, teaching me that it's okay to ask questions, okay to get angry, and also okay if I didn't please everyone all the time. And he was teaching me that it was wrong to allow the men in my life, including Jack, to be the judges by whose opinions I measured my successes or failures.

Still, I didn't want to be late. There was no sense in testing those theories right then. It was a hard habit to break after more than thirty years.

I parked the car, walked into the party, and entered the diversion of noise and laughter. Loud music, loud conversation, people straining to hear and be heard, laughter and booze. For a half hour I mingled, wondering why I had rushed. I could have stayed at home and talked with Jody while he ate his ice cream. Then Jack arrived.

"Hi, honey, I'm sorry I'm late. The traffic was terrible coming up from Annapolis tonight."

"That's okay—I haven't been here long," I said, letting him know there was no problem and I wasn't upset because he was late.

As we moved through the crowd laughing and talking to those we passed, Jack's fingers slid between mine and folded tightly around my hand. A firm little squeeze brought our gaze together. The touch and the look sent a tingle through my body that settled in the lower part of my stomach.

"I wish we were going to be together tonight," I whispered as I leaned close to him and put my lips next to his ear.

"We are together," he teased.

"You know what I mean," I said with a laugh.

"I asked you to come back to my apartment," he said, indicating that the invitation was still open. "We could leave right now," he went on.

"I can't, not tonight. Let's get something to eat," I suggested as a way of changing the direction of our conversation, knowing I had started something I wasn't going to be able to finish.

At about ten-thirty I told Jack I was going to call Jody

and make sure everything was okay. I made my way up
the stairs from the club basement to the kitchen, where I
found a phone hanging on the wall. People were crowded
around the sink, and someone was getting ice out of the
freezer. It was noisy, but maybe if I held the phone tight
to my ear and covered the other ear with my hand, I could
hear. I dialed my number. The phone was ringing.

"Hello," he answered.

"Hi, Jody, it's me. How are things? What are you
doing?"

He said something, but I couldn't hear him, even
though I was straining to listen, huddled in a corner trying
to get away from the sounds of the party.

"What did you say? I couldn't hear you. It's pretty noisy
here. You know how parties are. Everyone thinks they have
to scream, and the music is so loud."

There was silence. This time I didn't even hear the
muffled tones of any words.

"Jody, are you there? Jody, do you hear me?"

The phone went dead. I heard a click, then a dial tone.

He had hung up. Jody had hung up on me. I was
stunned. He had never done anything like that before in
his life.

I dialed the number again. I heard ringing. No answer.
I hung up the phone and walked back downstairs to where
Jack was waiting at the bar. My heart was beating rapidly
as I tried to remain calm.

"Do you want another glass of wine?" he was asking me.

"I'm going home," I said.

"Why?" he asked.

"Jody just hung up on me. I couldn't hear him, and he
hung up on me. He's never done anything like that, ever."

"Do you want me to go with you?" Jack asked.

"No, no. I don't think so. I'll call you later."

"Okay, drive carefully, and let me know if everything is all right.

"I will. I'm sure it will be. I just don't understand."

I left without saying goodbye to anyone. I had to get home as quickly as I could.

All the way home I kept thinking, I don't understand. He's not that kind of kid. He's never done anything like that. He's never, ever, been rebellious about anything. All those times when his father had punished him, and I thought it was unfair, he'd taken it without a word. When he was five and six he had trouble developing his speech, and his father made him sit at the dinner table before an empty plate, threatening not to give him anything to eat until he properly pronounced the name of the food we were having. Jody never could do it, and I always stepped in and insisted that the child be fed without all that pressure.

My intervention always resulted in an argument between John and me. I hated arguments and would usually do anything to avoid them, but I couldn't stand watching my son be treated like that. It was John's theory that Jody's strange speech pattern and unusual pronunciations were due to laziness and that if he were forced to speak properly, he could do it. Experts who eventually examined Jody said that he had developed his own way of talking, and that it was a lazy speech pattern. But it took months of speech therapy with a highly trained specialist to help him get over the difficulty and enable him to speak so that people outside the family could understand him.

It was a very difficult time for Jody. When he started school, no one could understand him. The teachers were frustrated because when Jody raised his hand to answer a question and they called on him, they couldn't understand whether his answer was right or wrong. The other children in the class would laugh at him, and the teacher didn't know whether to make him repeat what he had said, subjecting him to further ridicule, or tell him to sit down.

For some reason, the laughter and lack of understanding didn't deter Jody from raising his hand in class. When he knew the answer, which was most of the time, up went the hand and out came the answer, but in gibberish. The kids in the car pool even made fun of him by speaking what they called "Jody-talk." For example: "The own ow its on a een eeld" said very fast. Translation: "The brown cow sits in a green field." It was frustrating and humiliating at times, and it almost broke my heart to watch what he had to go through. One day he was supposed to go to a friend's house after school, but the mother of the child had decided to get someone else to drive her car pool and had forgotten to tell that person that Jody White would be coming home with her child. Jody stood on the sidewalk outside the school trying to make the teachers understand that he *was* supposed to go home with his friend. But no one could understand what he was saying, and the woman driving the car pool knew nothing about picking him up.

I was called at home after all the children had left and no one had come to get Jody. When I got to the school my little six-year-old was standing on the sidewalk with tears of frustration in his eyes, afraid that he had done something wrong and that I would be upset because he hadn't been able to carry out the plans we had made. I cried all the way home, and that's when I decided we'd get a speech therapist, no matter what it cost.

During those times at the table when his father was trying to force him to speak by withholding his food, Jody never cried or voiced a complaint, either then or later. Never did he speak out against punishment of any kind, no matter how unjust, no matter how large or small; he went along with it and made the best of it. I suppose he had followed my example, doing what he had seen me do in my relationship with his father. He had always been so passive. That's why this action with the phone call so disturbed me.

He must really be hating me tonight. Why had I gone to that dumb party? Why had I left him alone? Did Jody think that I had turned my back on his father because of Jack and that now Jack was taking me away from him? Please, dear God, make him all right, and I'll never go out again.

Why was I so afraid? What was I afraid I'd find when I got home? It was in the back of my mind, but I refused to let myself think it, as if by thinking that my son might do what his father had done could make it happen.

I parked the car and ran into the house. There were no lights on in the den, so I figured Jody must be upstairs in his room. I bounded up the steps, rounded the corner at the top of the landing, and ran up the first section of steps to the third floor. The door on the landing was closed. Jody never closed that door. I turned the door knob. The door was locked. I'd forgotten there was a lock on that door. Panic rushed through me.

"Jody," I called out, trying to control my voice but speaking loudly enough for him to hear me through the closed door and up another half flight of stairs.

"What are you doing? Why is this door locked?"

Silence.

"Jody," I screamed, the panic no longer under control. "Open this door, *now*."

"Go away. I don't want to talk to you."

He's alive, I thought. The tears of relief rolled down my face. Thank you, dear God, thank you. Jody must have heard the terror in my voice, and though he might be angry with me, he wouldn't want to cause me the kind of anguish he must have heard when I screamed out.

I heard him walk down the steps to the landing. I heard the sound of the lock being opened, then the thudding of his feet running up again as I opened the door. As I started up the steps after him I saw him dive back into bed, pull the covers around his head, and turn his face to the wall.

I sat down on the bed. "Jody, turn over, I want to talk to you."

"Leave me alone," he said. "You don't want to be here anyway."

The fear that had enveloped me was giving way to frustration and anger. Jody brought a special kind of joy into my life. The girls knew he was special to me. He was my baby, and I always felt extra protective toward him. Besides, there seemed to be that certain chemistry between us that makes any relationship special. Jody knew I worshiped the ground he walked on, and now he was accusing me of not wanting to be there, of not caring about him. I had just spent thirty minutes of sheer terror wondering if he would be all right when I got home, and he said I didn't want to be there—in essence, that I didn't care about him.

I grabbed the covers he was holding around his face and ripped them out of his hands. I took hold of his shoulders and pulled him over to face me.

"I want to talk to you, and I want you to look at me," I said, fresh tears running down my already tear-streaked face. Tears also flooded the eyes of my son as he looked into my face and listened as I choked out my message.

"I love you, Jody, and there isn't anywhere else on earth I would rather be than with you. But I'm an adult, and I'm going to want to spend time socializing with other adults, and that means Jack. We can't always be together. Before long you're not even going to want to be with me. In a few years you'll have a girl friend, and I'll have to force you to spend time with your old mom." I smiled through the tears, and he smiled back.

"I know you miss your father terribly and it's lonely for you without him." It was the first time I'd mentioned the pain John's death must be causing Jody, and a look of revelation came across his face.

"I also know it's scary in this house at night alone, especially since your father killed himself here. It must have been very frightening for you here tonight."

The tears flowed from my son's eyes once again. I had hit another sensitive spot. He had been frightened. Perhaps there were thoughts of a ghost, perhaps strange sounds, real or imagined.

"You don't have to be fourteen to have such feelings. I've had them myself." I didn't say that out loud, but I wish I had said it. I wish I had taken the sharing that one step further so Jody would understand that adults too get frightened of the real and the imagined. I also wish I hadn't done all the talking. I wish I had said, "What were you feeling tonight? Was it scary? Were you missing your father a lot? Did you hate me for leaving you alone?" It's one thing to let a child know you understand what he's

going through, but it's also very important—perhaps more important—for him to verbalize those thoughts and feelings. Problems become magnified when they are not talked about, becoming almost too big to handle. When we discuss them they're shared and reduced to a manageable size.

I looked down at Jody, almost fifteen years old but still needing my protection. How I hated to see him hurt. I'd bear any amount of pain if he could just be spared any more suffering, I thought.

"I won't let another night like tonight happen," I told him. "Someone will either be here with you or you'll visit a friend's house or I won't go out. And don't ever think I don't want to be with you. I love you."

I reached down and took my baby in my arms and hugged the little boy I hadn't hugged five years earlier when I'd told him I was leaving his father. Here we were five years later: the same room, the same frightened young boy trying to be brave, and more pain. But things would be different now. There was nothing and no one to stop me from making him forget all the pain of the past and protecting him from any more in the future. Jody had been through so much in his young life. I ached for the insecurities he must have been suffering; I imagined how alone he must have felt that night, and I hated myself for causing his unhappiness. I'd have done anything to undo those couple of hours, which must have seemed interminable as he sat feeling frightened and thinking no one cared. Did he have any idea how much I really loved him, I wondered. If anything ever happened to Jody, I don't know what I'd do, I thought. I wanted to make it up to him. I wanted to make my baby feel "all better." And I knew only one way to do that. When as a little boy he'd hurt himself, I'd pick him up, kiss the injury, and give him something to make him smile and take his mind off the problem.

"Did you eat that TV dinner?" I asked.

"No," he said, rolling his head back and forth on the pillow and wiping away the tears and his runny nose with his sheet.

"I didn't think so," I said. "I bet you didn't even eat the chocolate chip ice cream, did you?"

"No."

"Well, forget the TV dinner—how about an Egg Mc-White before we have a big dish of that ice cream?"

"Okay," he said, smiling.

I got up from the bed and walked downstairs to prepare my specialty (a variation of McDonald's Egg McMuffin). The kids were so used to calling them Eggs McWhite, they actually started asking for them by that name at Mc-Donald's. I first began fixing these especially for Jody. He liked them from the very first bite. Whenever I wanted him to know he was special to me, that I cared about him, I'd fix him an Egg McWhite—my token of love.

I stood at the stove fixing the egg, and when I heard Jody walk into the kitchen, I turned to face a different child.

"How long do you think it will take me to get my expert rating on the 125 motorcycle?" he asked cheerfully.

"Well, you know as well as I do you have to win so many points in the C class and then the same number in the B class before you can move up to the A class and expert," I answered.

"Well, I bet you I can get through C faster than anyone else has done it," he boasted.

"Don't be so sure," I said, trying to tease and temper

his "better than anyone else" attitude but delighted to see this positive push, this outgoing drive to be the best.

What a difference a few hours can make—and a tearful, honest outpouring of emotions and feelings! I told myself that Jody now knew how I felt and that he was reassured.

It was my typical "I want everything to be all right, therefore it will be" illusion.

Jody's mood had changed. I had soothed his feelings for the moment. But what I had really done was merely put a Band-Aid on an open sore.

Jody needed serious attention, deep and thorough probing. His emotional wounds needed to be completely cleansed so that he could heal with little or no scar tissue. I didn't really solve or resolve anything in those few minutes. I made him feel temporarily better, which made me feel better.

CHAPTER 5

A YEAR OF SUNSHINE
SPRING 1975 THROUGH SPRING 1976

ODY was happy that year, almost carefree. I never saw him depressed.

His friends from school as well as his motorcycle buddies were around a lot. He was doing extremely well in school and he was proud of every report card. I saw a fun-loving, seemingly well-adjusted teenager, and my heart filled with joy. I felt my prayers had been answered; Jody had not only adjusted to the loss of his father but was well on his way to being his own person. At this point I had reason to believe in the power of love and positive thinking.

Jody did move through the C class of 125 cc amateur moto-cross racing on the East Coast in near record time. He won every race he entered, accumulating the necessary points quickly to move on to the B class. Every Sunday I watched with pride and shared in his joy. He was beginning to take the thrill of victory for granted and was full of himself as only a young person can be when he believes in himself and his abilities and sees those abilities produce positive results.

The B class, however, wasn't quite so easy for him, and the humility that losing produces returned, at least in part, to my overzealous son. But it was a very good year on the moto-cross circuit for him and for me. Each Sunday began about 6:00 A.M. with the loading of the motorcycles on the trailer. Usually one or two of Jody's friends went with us, which made the drive of an hour or more to various tracks a lot more fun. There would be a stop for doughnuts on the way to the track and a stop on the way back, at night, for hamburgers or pizza. And then there was the picnic I would pack to be eaten at the track between motos. There was laughter and camaraderie between Jody and his friends. That included good-natured kidding as well as the strong competition between them.

It was a year of growth for the boys individually and as a group. They would do everything possible to beat each other during a race, but they'd spend the whole time between motos helping each other fix a bike if one broke down. They shared the kind of relationship that binds teenagers together, the kind that is deep and lasting, that guides and influences. It was the kind of relationship that can cause problems for parents if a conflict develops between what the group thinks is right and what Mom and Dad dictate.

Thank God, they were all good kids from good, caring families, and, thank God, the kids liked me, and I loved them. Several called me Mom, and they had accepted me as a moto-crossing mama. I was very lucky. They had all known John and had gone to the races with him. He had been a mechanic, the one to fix the kids' bikes. But they accepted me, accepted my Eggs McWhite and fried chicken in place of John's talents with motorcycle tools. They did everything possible to make me feel comfortable, and they succeeded. I was one of the gang, and I loved it.

In addition to the Sunday race routine, there were wonderful Saturdays around the farm. The kids would ride their motorcycles through the woods and around the fields. They even set up a practice moto-cross course in the hillside pasture. Occasionally I would get *my* motorcycle out and go riding with the kids. It was what I analyzed as my death-defying effort to hold onto my youth and stay close to my son. Even though it could be dangerous, and I had accumulated my share of injuries, including a couple of broken ribs, I did enjoy riding through the woods with the kids. With the exception of the deafening sound of the motorcycle engine, it is somewhat like horseback riding in the woods, which I enjoyed during my childhood. There's a sense of freedom, or perhaps I should say a reduction of restrictions, you feel when you roar down a trail, round a bend, splash through a mountain stream, climb a bank, hop a log, and float through a field of tall grass. The power is at the fingertips of the hand that controls the throttle. You have the ability to speed up and feel a surge of power and motion or slow down and watch the sun flare through the trees.

For me there were limits on how fast I could go and still control the bike or how slowly and still maintain my balance. For the kids, the moto-cross racers, there appeared to be no limits, no unconquerable challenges in trail riding. No banks were too steep, no hills too high, no logs too big to ride up or over at any speed they chose.

So it was impossible for me to keep up with the boys, and it was Jody's particular pleasure to tease me by racing off ahead to a bend in the trail, where he would jump off his motorcycle, lean it against a tree, take off his helmet, and sit on the ground to wait for me as if he had been there for hours. I would come down the trail riding as hard and as fast as I could, not wanting to be a slowpoke, ruining the boy's ride, or to get lost. I would round the bend, and there he'd be, all relaxed, leaning back against the tree. He'd shrug his shoulders and raise his hands in a gesture that asked, "What took you so long?" I'd either stop to catch my breath while we exchanged some good-natured verbal jabs or I'd ride by as fast as I could, giving Jody a "Ha-ha, very funny" as I flew by. (Well, it felt like flying to me.) He would, of course, catch up to me and pass me in a matter of seconds.

These rides were special to me, and I know they were special to Jody, because many times, without my asking, he would get my motorcycle out of the shed, check the oil, gas it up, and get it ready for a ride. He'd tell me it was time to hit the trail and would not accept my protests that I had too many other things to do.

The motorcycles proved to be a link that brought us closer together than ever before. It's ironic, because when John and Jody started riding motorcycles, I didn't want anything to do with them. Motorcycles scared me, and I felt very uncomfortable on one. I found no pleasure at all in accidentally turning on the throttle too fast and having that powerful machine pop out from under me and, in many cases, fall over on me. But now, with Jody, it was all different. For one thing, I had learned to master the machine, because I now had a reason to.

We spent many, many hours together with motorcycles as the excuse. In warm weather we went on motorcycle picnics. We packed sandwiches and soft drinks in a knapsack carried on the back as we rode through the woods to our favorite spot, where the land juts out into the reservoir. The tall pines offered shade on a hot summer day, and the blanket of pine needles provided a sweet-smelling bed on which to stretch out ourselves and spread out our food. There were no problems on those picnics, no pressures. There was bright sunlight, and calm waters. There were stones to skip and no clocks to watch. Just a mother and her son without any outside interference.

Such time spent together, moments to remember, don't just happen—they have to be made. There were also special moments in the cold of winter. One particular snowy day Jody gave us his version of the horse and sleigh. It was a snow saucer tied with heavy rope behind the motorcycle. Since he was lighter than I, it was decided he would ride in the saucer first while I drove the motorcycle, pulling him behind me. We started out just fine down a straight stretch in one of the pastures. But when we got to the end of the field, and I tried to turn, the saucer slid out to the side, unbalancing the bike and pulling me and the motorcycle over on our sides. I wasn't going fast enough to be hurt. I just sort of toppled over, awkwardly, into the snow. Jody loved it. He laughed—oh, how he laughed. The giggle of that wonderful carefree little boy he had once been a long, long time ago echoed across the pasturelands and through the woods on that snowy January day. When he drove the motorcycle and I rode in the saucer, this never happened. No matter how hard I tried to do what he had done, his superb balance and ability to handle a motorcycle countered my weight and efforts to upset him. By shifting his weight, standing up, leaning over, and accelerating at just the right moment, Jody prevented me from ever pulling him over. This also delighted him.

I'd yell, "I'll get you this time," but I never did.

He'd laugh and I'd laugh and say, "Next time I'll get you—you just wait. You'll be sorry for all those times you dumped me in the snow. You're going to wish you'd never come up with this idea."

It was wonderful, a wonderfully warm winter day for Jody and me. There were many wonderful days that year, days that made me feel confident that life could and would be very good to us from now on. Jody was making my hopes and dreams for the future come true that year.

Jody took over many of John's former responsibilities, doing them as well as his father had. We got the swimming pool operating for the first time on our own—no easy task, I might say. We cleaned and painted the pool, and, most important, we got the old filter system started up, an accomplishment that brought Jody running from the basement to announce success. The lawn-cutting chores were shared by all of us. We even mended a few fences and got the old homestead in pretty good shape.

Marjorie had returned from Africa with many exciting stories. I'm glad I didn't know about them when they were happening. O'Donnell was going into her senior year, and I decided that if she wanted to live on campus her last year, it would be all right with me. Marjorie was going to start college in New England, and that would leave Jody to share late week-night dinners with me. He'd stay at his cousin's house after school, and I'd pick him up after work. There would still be much time for us together during the Sunday moto-cross races and while doing Saturday chores and taking rides around the farm. I felt it would all work out okay.

In addition to our adjusting, getting it together without John, Jack and his young son Christopher, now six, were beginning to adopt our way of life. They would come out to the farm to swim in the pool, play in the snow, roll in piles of freshly raked leaves, and walk through the fields to pick black-eyed Susans and wild daisies. There were dinners and movies and nights at home watching TV, and occasionally they would join us at the moto-cross races.

Jack and I even managed to have some time to ourselves to nourish our passion and romance. But what stands out in my memory about that year was the blending of our two families and our two entirely different life-styles. Jack, born and raised in the city, was learning to accept the unrestricted country existence I had known all my life, one with fewer conveniences but many more freedoms. At first Jack and Christopher were timid about some of the new experiences, but they eventually learned to respect and often to enjoy those activities we considered routine.

But motorcycles they couldn't handle, nor were they entirely comfortable with gentle farm animals, which seemed big and somewhat intimidating to a little boy and even to a man who had been raised with only a pet dog. The sleds went a little too fast on the steep, snowy hills of the rolling countryside, not at all like the gentle slopes in a city park. The bugs were a nuisance, the snakes frightening, the dark, still nights a little too still; no neighbors, no traffic, no noise except the constant cricket concert from dusk to dawn. To top it off, the lushness of nature aggravated the allergies from which both Jack and Christopher suffer. But we were being drawn closer and closer together, closer than I had ever thought possible. We were sharing and growing individually, as a couple, and as two families that could very easily be one.

Occasionally, at the end of a hot summer day when the long-lasting daylight still lingered and the heat was just as persistent, Jack and Christopher and I would walk down to the lake to watch Jody and his friends dive off high rocks into the dark, forbidding waters of the reservoir—a daring feat that brought oohs and aahs from me, warnings of danger from Jack, and wide-eyed stares from six-year-old Christopher as he held tightly to his father's hand.

Jody loved showing off, loved being brave, loved doing something he knew Jack wouldn't do, and he loved to impress Christopher by being macho. He wanted to be special to Jack and his son, and this was his way of getting their attention. He once said to me after a badly ridden motorcycle race which Jack had watched, "I always lose when Jack's here. He's never seen me win." I told him Jack didn't care. He just enjoyed watching him ride. But I don't think I convinced him. Jody knew that his father had always wanted him to do well, so I guess he thought the only way he could impress Jack was by winning. Unfortunately, we didn't talk about it and make it clear to Jody that Jack wasn't like that, that not all men demanded perfection as payment for affection.

The other thing that bothered me was that there wasn't much interaction between Jack and Jody. I was their go-between. Jack was concerned about being too forward with Jody. He was afraid that Jody would think he was trying to replace John as his father. I think Jody wanted his father replaced. He wanted another man in his life who would care about him. Jack held the key to a good relationship between them, but he didn't know it. He is a good communicator. He could have answered many of Jody's needs by talking to him. But Jack thought that because he didn't ride a motorcycle or ski or swim very well, they had nothing in common. I did everything Jody did— rode motorcycles, skied, and was a good swimmer; as a matter of fact, I was a competition swimmer. And still Jack and I found an important common ground on which to develop a deep relationship that had nothing to do with those activities.

Jack and I shared some interests, but what brought us so close together was honest, open communication and understanding. Jack taught me to say what was on my mind, to open up about what I was thinking and feeling, to express myself to another person without fear of being judged. Jack shared his emotions with me and encouraged me to do the same with him. He taught me to be more than just pleasant on every and all occasions. He taught me that it's okay to be angry and show it. Jody longed for the same kind of a relationship. He needed it desperately. Jack had the ability to give my son what he craved, what no one else had been able to give him, but he didn't know it and he was too shy to reach out. I didn't realize it at the time, and Jody was much too shy and too inept at talking about his feelings to express those needs. And so they went unmet, unfulfilled, lying dormant beneath the surface of this teenager looking for someone who would understand, feel, and share with him, someone who would listen and say, "I know how you feel; I felt the same way when I was your age."

There was one person who did some special sharing with Jody that year. Without talking about the problems and pain caused by Jody's father killing himself, this person showed as much care and understanding as anyone who hasn't been through such an experience can. But what she did for Jody more than anything else was to lead him away from his pain by spending time with him, making him laugh, and, more than anyone in Jody's world, making him feel he was not facing life alone. Lisa Niner was barely thirteen years old, but she had the insight and sensitivity of someone much older. A very petite child, thin and straight, with almost no hint of the womanhood ahead that would bring rounded hips and breasts, she had a small chiseled face and eyes that danced with a devilish dare. Lisa was a motorcycle buddy, and when she was wearing racing leathers and a helmet, no one took her for a girl. Even without her helmet it was hard to tell. Her hair was usually cut short, but in that era of long-haired boys, even when she let it grow she was still mistaken for a boy. She must have heard people refer to her as "him" a thousand times, but she never got used to it, and she always fought for feminine recognition.

The relationship between Jody and Lisa began to deepen almost immediately after John's death. She went to Jacksonville for the National Youth Moto-Cross with us, and it was then that the friendship started to become something more. I realized driving back from Florida that young love was blooming in the back seat of my car, right behind my back, and I was delighted. I'd hear a giggle, and, glancing into the rear-view mirror, I'd see that shy look of love on those two fresh, innocent faces, unscarred by previous romance gone wrong, the newness of the feeling openly showing in their unguarded expressions. They were wrapped in a blanket, to keep warm, they said, but I could see by the outline of the cover that they were holding hands. I smiled, looked away from the mirror, and turned the radio up to provide some privacy for their whispers and laughs.

Lisa started coming to the house to visit more often. Sometimes I'd pick her up on the way home from work on Friday, and she'd spend the weekend. They'd ride motorcycles and swim, play card games, and generally have a very good time. They even played with little Christopher when he came out with Jack, kidding with him, riding him on their shoulders. He loved it, and so did the rest of us. Laughter and noise from happy kids had erased the gloom in the old farmhouse.

At times Jody and Lisa remained alone when I went out with Jack. Most of the time O'Donnell was there, but not always. I probably shouldn't have allowed that, but I trusted them completely, and I didn't feel they were ready to experiment with sex. They never gave me reason to believe I had made a mistake. They were good kids and good company for each other, and, after the incident when I left Jody by himself, I was glad Lisa was there.

As much as I loved Lisa—and I still do—when I look back I wonder if I wasn't using her occasionally to relieve me of my responsibilities with Jody. I knew Jody enjoyed her company; he was very happy when she was there. But not only was I delighted to have my son share time with someone he really wanted to be with, I was also being given the opportunity to go off and do what I wanted to do. And I wonder if my doing that made Jody feel he was being pushed into adulthood. He had his friend and I had my friend, and we each did our own thing. Did he think I wanted him to stop being a child and grow up? Did it look as though I preferred him to be a friend and equal rather than my son? Certainly I was sending a message to him that I enjoyed being out, not worrying about being home and being a mother. There was even one time when I caused our roles to be completely reversed.

It was a Friday night. I had picked up Lisa after work, grabbed something at the store for her and Jody's dinner, and rushed home. (By preparing their dinner and not making them do it themselves I made myself feel I wasn't neglecting my duties as a parent.) As soon as I had fixed that dinner I raced out again, telling the kids that I wouldn't be late and asking them to wait up for me.

I hurried off to a party given by our friends Andy and Toba Barth, twenty-five miles away in Columbia, Maryland. Jack was going to meet me there. No lunch, a late dinner, and too much wine combined to make me intoxicated very quickly. The Barths insisted that I spend the night, and I didn't resist. Toba called Jody and told him I was spending the night there and not to worry. I woke up on the sleep sofa in the Barths' living room about six o'clock Saturday morning fully dressed except for my shoes. Jack was asleep beside me. He had taken my shoes off, and now I couldn't find them. My head ached excruciatingly when I bent over to see if the shoes were under the sofa bed. So I said the heck with it, grabbed my coat, and, in the cold winter dawn, ran in stockinged feet to my car and headed for home.

When I got there I jumped out of the car and ran quietly down the cold flagstone path to the front door. I opened the door as softly as possible so as not to wake the kids. (Picture the old cartoon of the husband sneaking in after a late night with the boys, holding his shoes in his hand—except that I didn't have any shoes.) I carefully closed the front door and looked over in the direction of the den. There were Lisa and Jody sitting on the sofa staring at me, wide awake, as if they hadn't been to sleep at all. They started laughing and chattering. My son and his girl friend had waited up for me.

"You told us not to go to bed until you came home," Jody said.

"What did you do with your shoes?" Lisa asked. She would notice, I thought.

"I couldn't find them when I went to leave, and I didn't want to wake up the Barths by looking for them."

"Can you imagine coming home without your shoes?" Jody asked incredulously.

"It's something you'd better not do," I warned. "I got sick—it must have been something I ate."

"Sure, Mom."

"Well, okay. I was very, very tired after a hard week at work, and I drank too much wine. I should have known better, but that's what happened. Now I'm going to bed, in my own bed, and you guys better do the same. Jody upstairs, Lisa in Marjorie's room."

I'd left them there all night, and now I was making sure they went to separate beds. Great mother you are, Susan, I thought to myself, and what a fine example you're setting by getting drunk and sneaking in without your shoes at six-thirty in the morning. I have been drinking too much lately, I thought to myself, ever since John's death. That's no excuse, and booze is no way to deal with your problems. It just makes a difficult life more difficult, I lectured myself on the way up the stairs and into bed. I would try to be better.

CHAPTER 6

A TIME OF CHANGE
JUNE 1976

*T*HE bacon on the stove was spitting at me, the phone was ringing, and Jody was revving up the engine of his motorcycle right outside the kitchen window. Whatever has happened to the peace and quiet of the country? I grabbed the phone.

"Hello," I said with little patience.

"Hello," came a small female voice on the other end of the line. "Is Jody there?"

It was not Lisa. It was not a voice I'd ever heard before. "Oh, he's out working on his motorcycle, but maybe I can call him to the phone. May I tell him who's calling?"

"This is Lauren. I'm a friend of his."

"Oh, okay, just a minute. I'll see if he can come to the phone."

I walked to the back door, opened it, and yelled to be heard above the motorcycle.

"Jody, someone's on the phone for you."

I waved my hands at the same time, so that even if he

didn't hear me, he might see me and know that I was trying to talk to him. He pushed the kill button, and the
engine died. It was quiet again. I stopped shouting and
returned to a normal tone of voice.

"There's someone on the phone for you. She says her
name is Lauren and she's a friend of yours."

"Ugh—tell her I'm not here."

"Okay, I'll just tell her you're too busy to come to the
phone."

"Tell her I'll never come to the phone when she calls.
She's a little pest. Tell her to get lost."

"I'll tell her you're too busy to come to the phone. If
you want to tell her all the rest of that, you can do it yourself."

"Hello, Lauren. Jody is working on his bike right now
and he can't come to the phone."

"Can I call later? What would be a good time?" she
asked.

"Well, he's not going to be home much today. Maybe
you might want to try tonight."

"Okay," she said in a cheery voice, not sounding a bit
discouraged. "Bye."

I hung up just as Jody was walking into the kitchen.

"What did you tell her?"

"I told her you were too busy to come to the phone, but
you're going to have to talk to her sometime. She's obviously going to keep calling, so you better decide what to
say to her before she calls again. Who is she?" I asked.

"Just some girl. She goes to Eddie's school, and she's
always hanging out at Patty's. Patty lives next door to
Eddie."

"Well, she sounded like a very nice girl," I said for no
particular reason.

"She's a brat, a pest, just a little kid." Jody was trying to convince me or maybe himself that he had absolutely no interest in little Lauren.

"Well, here's your breakfast—a feast fit for the world's newest ladies' man. Paul Newman and Robert Redford have nothing on Jody White—girls calling all the time, just dying to hear the sound of your voice or catch a glimpse of you at a friend's house or on the moto-cross course. Probably thousands of girls will flock to the race this Sunday just to see the famous Jody White."

"Sure, Mom. Couldn't I just have some orange juice, please?"

I was teasing Jody, but as I looked at his handsome face and well-built body, his strong shoulders, I knew he would get many calls from girls before he settled on *the one* to be his wife—which I hoped would be many years from then. This, I thought, is just the first of a lot of phone calls to come from girls pursuing my son. When I was a teenager girls didn't call boys, but that's all changed now, and I'm sure Jody will be one of those who either benefits from the change or is pestered to death by it. In any case, the girls will never give him reason to doubt his attractiveness. And that may be important for someone as shy as he is.

Lauren did continue to call, and Jody *did* talk to her. She also showed up at the motorcycle races, usually with several other girls. My joke about girls flocking to the track was exaggerated but accurate. The girls would crowd around Jody before and after a race, talking excitedly and laughing about everything and nothing at all.

The first time I saw Lauren I thought she looked even younger than Lisa. A tiny girl, she was thin and flat-chested and couldn't have weighed more than seventy-five or eighty pounds. Her brown hair was smartly cut in a style that flattered her small face and big eyes. Her eyebrows were plucked in an arch, and she wore makeup, which she probably thought made her look older. But I always thought she looked like a little girl playing dress-up with her mother's cosmetics. There's no question, though, that she was cute and bouncy and probably very appealing to the boys—Jody included—despite his earlier complaints about her.

As Lauren was moving into Jody's life Lisa was moving out—not by choice but because of circumstances. She had begun to go in for a different kind of motorcycle racing, something called flat track, or short track. It involves a flat oval track and is more like regular motorcycle racing, in which speed and maneuvering for position are more important than the physical strength and agility needed for moto-cross. Those races were held at tracks other than those used for moto-cross and took place primarily on Saturday nights. So Lisa was racing at one place on Saturday, and Jody raced at another place on Sunday. Their paths began to separate, barely crossing at all anymore.

Occasionally Lisa would come to a Sunday moto-cross race, but Jody was not as warm as he once was, and it hurt her to see the other girls laughing and talking to Jody and his friends. All of a sudden she felt like an outsider. She hadn't changed, her feelings were the same, but someone had come between her and Jody. There was nothing she could do about it but accept the loss as part of growing up, a very painful part.

Lisa had shared something very special with Jody, and she had been there when he needed someone to turn to for understanding and closeness. What she had experienced with him would always remain with her. He was her first love. She was his. But memories fall sadly short when compared to spending time with someone you care about, and she would miss doing that with Jody. She would miss it very much. And so would I. Lisa was good for Jody. People we meet during our lifetimes have varying effects on us. Some bring out the positive in our personalities, some the negative, some a little of both. Lisa Niner had only a positive influence on Jody. He was happier, more outgoing, more full of fun and had a sharper wit when Lisa was around. I was sorry to see him lose her friendship and stimulus. And I would miss having her around. She had become part daughter and part sister to me. I would even miss her walking up to me and saying, "Hi, Mom. I see you're wearing your shoes today."

Sometimes parents try to choose their children's friends and even husbands or wives. I never did, but if I could have had a say, Lisa would have been my choice for Jody. However, teen years are rarely spent pursuing parental wishes. More often it seems that the passionate pastime of adolescents is to find out what their mothers and fathers would like and do the exact opposite.

It is the way of nature, I would tell myself. Otherwise kids would never become independent. But I really didn't want my children to leave home, and I wanted to spare them some of the pain of those difficult changing years. I wanted them to listen to my warnings so they could avoid at least a few of the pitfalls awaiting teenagers. There is no way you can watch a child you love more than your own life heading toward a dangerous precipice and let him walk over it without trying to stop him.

One day I was standing in the laundry room putting clothes in the washing machine when I glanced out the window at Jody and a boy from down the road. They were at the top of the lawn, about a hundred feet away under the maple tree, sitting astride their motorcycles. The boy was not in Jody's regular group of friends, he was just another kid who was into motorcycles. Everybody knew Jody raced, and the boy had ridden up to ask how to register and get started in moto-cross racing. They were just sitting there talking when this kid took a package out of his shirt pocket, pulled out what looked like a cigarette, lit it with a match, and started smoking. He puffed on it a couple of times, then took it between his thumb and forefinger, pulled it out of his mouth, and offered the unlit end to Jody. My heart skipped a beat, and I could feel my face flush as I waited to see what my son would do. Jody didn't smoke tobacco, and I knew by the way that cigarette had been offered that it was marijuana. I didn't know anything about pot and I didn't want to. I knew only that it was an illegal drug, and the thought of Jody getting mixed up with it terrified me.

Two years earlier I had discovered that Marjorie was smoking pot and I had panicked, crying and carrying on and making her promise not to smoke anymore until after her high school graduation.

"Please don't mess up your mind. Please give yourself a chance to think rationally about what you're doing," I had begged. She acted as if I were being silly and overreacting, but she agreed. She promised then, but two years later I wasn't sure whether or not she had gone back to smoking pot. I strongly suspected she had, but I was afraid to ask, afraid I'd hear the answer I didn't want to hear.

Jody's sixteen years old, and I'm not going to let him get into drugs, I told myself as I stood there waiting for him to accept the pot or turn it down. He casually shook his head no, and the other guy withdrew his extended arm and brought the cigarette back to his mouth. I released the breath I'd been holding. "Thank God," I muttered to myself. "Good for you, Jody." He knows how I feel about pot and he is respecting my wishes, I thought. But I'm still going to say something, I vowed. I'm not going to let this slide, not the way I did with Marjorie.

When the boy on the motorcycle left, I walked out the back door, across the lawn, and up to the spot under the maple tree where Jody was now tightening the chain on his bike.

"Hi," I said as if I were beginning a conversation with a stranger.

"Hi," he repeated, looking up at me as if to say, "Why are you acting so weird?"

"Who was that?" I asked.

"I don't know, somebody named Kevin. He just wanted to see if I had an AMA moto-cross registration form. I told him he could get one at C&L Cycle. He said that he wants to start racing and might want to buy my bike. If he buys my bike, can I get a new one?"

"I don't know, Jody, maybe. It's a lot of money that I don't have right now. Even if you sell this bike for a couple of hundred, the new one you want is almost a thousand."

"But all the top riders get a new bike every year, some a couple a year."

"But they have sponsors. You don't," I pointed out.

"It's going to be hard to compete without a new bike, almost impossible," he argued.

"We'll see," I said, and then, jumping into the subject I would have preferred to avoid, I blurted out, "I caught a glimpse of Kevin's cigarette. Was that pot?"

"Yeah," Jody admitted.

I spouted out everything I was thinking all at once. "I wasn't spying on you, but I saw him offer you some. I'm really glad you turned it down. I asked you before to promise me you wouldn't smoke marijuana, and I'm glad you're not. You know I'm not here all the time, so I'm glad I can trust you to keep your promise. I just can't deal with that added worry of your getting into pot. There's just too much to do and think about without that additional burden. Please don't let me down on this, Jody. You have to be stronger than other teenagers, stronger than some of your friends. You have to be able to say no and go on saying no. Okay?"

"Okay, Mom, I know and I won't," he reassured me.

"I really have to rely on your strength. We're not going to make it if we don't all pull together and help one another and respect each other's wishes," I said, pleading with him as if he had taken the pot.

"I know, Mom, I know." He sounded as if I were the child and he were the adult patiently putting up with my inane chatter.

"You've made me feel much better," I said with relief. "Why don't we go over to C&L and just see what a new bike would cost? Maybe they'll give you more for a trade-in than you could get by selling your bike to Kevin or anyone else."

I suppose it sounded like a bribe or a reward, and maybe it was. If Jody didn't add to my worries I would make life more pleasant for him by buying him something he wanted. I didn't mean it to be a bribe. I was relieved, and I wanted to celebrate. I had always gained much pleasure from giving the children things. It warmed my heart to watch their faces brighten with delight over a new toy or a piece of clothing or little gift they didn't expect, given

SUSAN WHITE-BOWDEN

*not for any special occasion but just because I like to make
them happy. But the gifts were getting bigger, and perhaps
I was using my buying power to try and buy their happiness, make up for the loss of their father, and ensure* my
freedom from worry. *If he were here, I thought many
times, they wouldn't have to do without. The truth is, it
was my peace of mind I was buying. I was so blinded by
my struggle to avoid having to deal with problems or
worries that I would have bought them the world if it
meant our lives would run problem-free.*

*John would never have allowed the kids to have as much
as I gave them. He firmly believed teenagers should work
for something as important as a motorcycle or a car. If
they didn't, he was convinced they wouldn't really appreciate its value and would abuse it, thus endangering themselves. I agreed with John on this issue, but I didn't follow
his wishes or my strong feelings that he was right. Instead
I adopted the attitude that it was just the kids and me now.
And I became less an authority figure and more a friend
and felt they should share whatever I had. They didn't
need to work for material things to appreciate them. They
understood I worked hard to get things, and they would
take care of them.*

*However, I think what I achieved with that philosophy
was to remove initiative and reduce the chances of allowing the kids, primarily Jody, to feel that wonderful sense
of worth and accomplishment that comes after working
and saving, sometimes for months or years, to get something you want. The personal rewards gained by such
sacrifice and accomplishments are far more important than
the material object that caused the desire and instigated
the effort. What you have acquired is the belief in your
ability to succeed, self-confidence, a feeling that if you*

133

can do it once you can do it many times, over and over again for a lifetime. And there is the independence you feel, the pride in having something that is really yours.

Many of us think our children will love us more if we give them all the things they want. I think that in the long run they love us less. If we provide our kids with their every wish, what is left for them to look forward to achieving in life? What do we leave them to dream about, to plan for when they're grown and, supposedly, earning their own way? I think the only thing we can't give too much of to children is our time and love.

Most of us make the mistake of trying to convert our love into such tangible things as toys and television sets, stereos and sports cars. We think that's the way to show our children how much we love them and care about them. But think back to your own childhood. What happy memory do you have of your relationship with your parents? Is it a time when they bought you something special or rather a special time when they did something for you or with you or maybe just talked with you when that was what you needed.

One morning early in June I was sitting on the side of the bed thinking that everything was going pretty well for the children and me at the time. O'Donnell had just graduated from high school and had been accepted at Wheelock College, in Boston. Marjorie was home for the summer; she would be going back to New England College in the fall, but at least for the summer Jody would have company at home during the day. Of course he was usually at a friend's house or his friends were over at our house. But I still felt better when one of the family was home, and Marjorie was the best of all. She ruled the nest with the strongest hand. "Where are you going, kid?" she'd say. "When will you be back? And don't be late."

It was one of those beautiful summerlike spring mornings. Now that Jody was out of school for the summer, I wasn't as rushed in the morning since I didn't have to leave so early. But sometimes, like this morning, I would savor the pleasure of not having to get an early start to such a degree that I would end up being late. I sat there putting off my departure and letting my thoughts wander. The scene from my bedroom window would have made a beautiful painting—the tall pasture grass reaching up to touch the incredibly blue sky, a few spring daisies and buttercups growing along the post-and-rail fence, adding a cheery, yellow accent to the bright green Maryland countryside.

The sweet scent of the blooming multiflora rose hedge drifted in through the open window. I was feeling really good sitting there enjoying the day, the season, the gift of life, overwhelmed with the human ability to absorb the beauties of nature and be emotionally moved by them.

Come fall Jody and I would have another year on our own, but he had his driver's license now, so he wouldn't be stranded at home so often when I wasn't around to drive him. In fact, I thought, O'Donnell wouldn't be able to have a car her first year at college, which meant the Honda I had just bought for her and Jody to share would be his alone to use while she was at school. I wondered if he'd thought about that and was sure he had. He certainly would have thought about *that,* I said to myself, smiling.

It would be convenient having Jody driving himself to and from school, but this past year had been rather pleasant—at least for me. And I thought the arrangement had been good for Jody. He had been going to his cousin Ricky

Watt's house after school, and I would pick him up after I got off the air, around seven forty-five. Jody complained about going there every day, even though he and Ricky were good friends. It wasn't Jody's house and family, and I think he felt he was in the way at times, although I'm sure he wasn't and I'm sure the Watts didn't make him feel he was. Jody was just that kind of child, a homebody. He sort of felt displaced, deprived, because he couldn't go to his home after school like every other kid in school. He refused to eat dinner with the Watts; instead he stayed upstairs and studied and waited for me to pick him up so we could have dinner together. But the drive home was good, just as the drive to school was. It gave us time to talk and to share our days.

Jody would tell me what went on at school, who said what in class, and who got demerits and why. Sometimes it was even he—never for any major offense. However, like most kids resisting rules and discipline, Jody would always have an excuse or complain that the school was too strict. "Can you imagine a school giving a demerit for throwing a snowball?" he'd say. "A little white, fluffy, harmless snowball?"

I'd tell him rules are rules, throw snowballs at home, not at school—but not at me, I'd add quickly. We'd laugh and I'd know there'd be a snowball battle between the two of us when we got home—and what's more, I looked forward to it.

Having his driver's license and a car the coming year would allow him to come home, but he'd be coming home to an empty house. Already I was worrying about that. Going to Ricky's house and waiting for me was much healthier. But, then, I thought selfishly, if I wanted to stay in town and have dinner with Jack, I could do that without having to worry about picking up Jody and driving him home.

I knew Jody was looking forward to being independent, to having his own wheels. It wasn't that aspect of the change that bothered me at that time. I felt sad to think we were growing apart, so I channeled my thoughts toward the advantages the change might have for me.

I was sitting there planning the year ahead when the phone rang and brought me abruptly back to the present.

"Hello."

I looked at the clock as I answered and realized I didn't have much time to talk.

"Hello, this is John Ordeman at St. Paul's. Mrs. White, we have a problem that involves Jody. A good many library cards were taken out of the backs of the books in our upper-school library, and when the custodian was cleaning out the lockers after the boys left school, he found them in the bottom of the locker assigned to Jody."

"I don't understand," I stammered, not quite sure how to handle the accusation.

"We're not sure, of course, that he put them there or took them, but I need to talk to him. Could you bring him to school or ask him to come to see me today?"

"Certainly," I said, "but there must be some mistake. I can't imagine that Jody would do such a thing—I can't think of any reason why he would. He's just not that kind of kid. He doesn't do anything to rock the boat or challenge authority. I'll talk to him right away and send him over to the school to clear this up."

I sat on the bed stunned for a moment. If he did take the cards out of the books, I thought, he wouldn't be dumb enough to leave them in the bottom of his own locker. This is ridiculous.

"Jody," I yelled from the bottom of the steps to the third floor. "Jody, come down here right away."

I heard him roll out of bed and start down the steps. I went back into my room and sat on the bed. I felt shaky, and I didn't want him to think I believed for a moment that he had done what the headmaster was suggesting. Jody walked into my room and stood before me. He was wearing a pair of cut-off jeans and a T-shirt. During the summer he slept in the same clothes he wore when he was awake. I wanted to hug him, not lecture him. I wanted to take him in my arms and protect him from any hurt or threat from those who didn't know my son as I knew him. But instead I tried to remain calm and keep my distance so he wouldn't have to deal with a whimpering, tearful mother in addition to an accusing headmaster.

"Mr. Ordeman was just on the phone. He said some library cards that have been missing were just found in the bottom of your locker. Do you know anything about this?"

"No," came Jody's fast and emphatic response. His face was blank.

"He says somebody took the cards from the backs of a lot of library books before school closed, and now they have all been found in the bottom of your locker."

"Somebody must have put them there," he said simply and believably.

"Well, will you please drive to school and tell Mr. Ordeman that? He says he must talk to you in person. Take Dean with you (Dean had been spending the night), but for heaven's sake, get this straightened out."

"Okay."

Jody turned and went back up to his room to change into clothes suitable for an audience with the headmaster.

He knew he should do that without my telling him. We're making progress, I thought. Jody usually relied on me to tell him what to wear for most occasions. I welcomed this sign that perhaps he was more secure about making such decisions on his own. Moments later I heard Jody and Dean clomping down the stairs from the third floor. I went into the hall as they reached the bottom of the steps.

"Get something to eat before you go," I said.

"We'll eat when we get back," Jody promised. "This shouldn't take very long."

"Will you call me at the station when you get home and let me know what's going on?"

"Sure," Jody said casually, making me believe there really was nothing to worry about.

I stopped thinking about the whole curious incident until the phone on my desk rang about three-thirty. I'd been out filming reports most of the day and had just gotten back. I answered, and Jody began to explain what had happened.

"Mr. Ordeman still thinks I was in on it," he began. His voice was quite without emotion.

"Why?" I asked.

"Well, he says three other guys told him that they had taken the cards and that I was with them. They said they did put the cards in my locker but that I was one of those who had taken them out of the library."

"What did you say?" I asked.

"I told him I didn't do it."

"What did he say?"

"He said the student honor board would be holding a hearing on it and the other three would be testifying that I did it. It would be their word against mine."

"What does that mean?" I asked.

"I guess it means I could get kicked out of school," he said casually, as if he were telling me we were out of milk.

"What!" I said with a great deal of concern and indignation. "They can't do that if you didn't do anything wrong. I'll call Mr. Ordeman. I'll get this straightened out," I said, confident that one phone call from me would get Jody off the hook and the matter settled. There was no question in my mind that my son was not guilty. If he was, he would have said so by now.

"I'll talk to you when I get home," I said, dismissing Jody and rather irately taking the situation into my own hands.

I hung up, looked up the number of the school, and picked up the phone again.

"May I speak to Mr. Ordeman?" I asked when the secretary answered.

"Certainly. May I tell him who's calling?"

"Susan White, Jody White's mother."

"Of course. Just a minute, Mrs. White."

"Hello"—Mr. Ordeman spoke softly into the phone, and I responded with a similar tone.

"This is Susan White. I've just talked to Jody and he told me that three of his classmates are accusing him of taking part in removing the library cards. But he still insists he didn't do it. However, he says if the honor board believes them instead of him, he could be expelled from school. Is that true?"

"It is, Susan, and I'll tell you why. The other boys have confessed that they did take the cards, and they swear that Jody was with them. If the honor board feels Jody is lying, he *will be* expelled. Lying is one thing that the school and the honor system, under which we operate, will not tolerate or forgive. If a student is caught lying, he must be expelled. The boys all know that. No matter what they do, if they admit it and don't lie when confronted, they will be punished but will be permitted to remain in school. Lying means immediate expulsion. I've talked to the other boys, and I'll be honest with you—I think Jody is lying. But I won't say that. It's up to the student board to make a decision on these charges. There is also another matter, which I didn't tell you about. Some metal fixtures on the chairs and also on the walls in the library were unscrewed and taken apart. And the boys said Jody did that also."

"Why would he?" I asked, still not believing any of this.

"I don't know. I wish I had some answers for you."

"I'll talk to Jody and try to get to the bottom of this," I said.

"The honor board is meeting tomorrow. I'll let you know what they decide," Mr. Ordeman concluded.

"Thank you," I said and hung up the phone.

Thank you for what, I thought. They don't care about Jody. All they care about is their honor board, their rules and regulations. If Jody lied about all this, something is really troubling him, and that's more important than their damned honor board. I don't believe it. I don't believe he is lying. Jody doesn't lie. He never has. He's not that kind of a child. Once when he was very small, about three or four, I told him he couldn't go out and play in the snow because it was too cold and blustery outside. That didn't mean anything to him. He still wanted to go out, much more than he wanted to obey me. But he didn't sneak out the door when I wasn't looking. Instead he put on his snow suit and boots and came and stood in front of me and said, "I'm going outside now," or, in his language, "m oing ide ow." As he watched my face for a reaction he moved toward the door repeating, "I'm going outside now." He was defying my order, but he was doing it in front of me. Unfortunately I eventually let him get away with it. With his hand on the doorknob, he said again, "I'm going outside now." His eyes searched my face for approval.

"No, you're not," I told him. "It's too cold out there."

The tears of disappointment started to roll down his cheeks, already rough and red from playing out in the cold winter wind. Those tears melted my parental control.

"Jody," I said, "you will stay inside until I get my snow clothes on, and then we'll go out together, okay?"

"Okay," he said with a smile that would have taken an Egyptian sun goddess out into a blizzard.

Discipline is important, and a child needs to be told no. Children have to learn that they can't have everything they want when they want it. Life is full of no's and disappointments and rejections. A child needs to begin dealing with that at an early age to be able to handle it later in life. I had a hard time saying no to Jody, and I know that left him inadequately prepared to accept no from others when he was older. I was doing him no favors by weakening and backing down when he took this kind of stand and used his little-boy charms to get his way.

But he did not lie or defy me behind my back. And I couldn't believe that he had now. And vandalism—no way would he be a party to that. Jody'd been taught to respect and take care of his own and other people's property. If he mistakenly brought home someone else's towel from the locker room at school, it would worry him until he returned it. There had to be a mistake about these charges against him. He just wouldn't do these things.

When I got home I found Jody up in his room lying on

the bed listening to music. He was staring at the ceiling, so he didn't see me when I walked in, and he certainly didn't hear me because the stereo was on so loud he wouldn't have heard a bomb blast. I stood in front of him.

"Could you turn that down, please?" I shouted. "I want to talk to you."

Jody got up slowly, walked the couple of steps to the stereo controls, turned the volume down, and went back to lie flat on his back again. He looked sullen and apprehensive, as if he knew what was coming.

"I called Mr. Ordeman after I talked to you on the phone," I began in my usual hesitant way when approaching an uncomfortable subject.

"And?" Jody questioned quietly, unchallenging.

"He believes that you're lying and the others are telling the truth. But he's not going to say so to the honor board. He will let them decide on their own. He also said that the other kids told him you dismantled some fixtures on the chairs and walls of the library, that you took a screwdriver to school and unscrewed the screws from these things."

Jody did not speak and he did not look at me. He just went on staring at the ceiling.

"Jody, please don't lie to me. Please tell me the truth. I don't care what you did, but I want to know the truth."

His head turned toward me and his eyes began to tear. He didn't speak, and once again I spoke for him.

"You did what they said, didn't you? But why?"

He looked so sad, so apologetic, hurt, as if he hadn't intended to cause so much trouble.

"It was just to mess up the librarian. She had given us a hard time this year, so we thought if we took the cards out of the back of the books, it would be a lot of extra work for her. I guess we thought it would be a good way to get even."

"And unscrewing the fixtures?" I asked.

"Just for something to do. I did it during study hall. The other guys bet me I couldn't do it without someone seeing me."

"Why did you lie about it, Jody? To do dumb things like that is not great, but lying made them much worse. Why didn't you just admit that you had done it, as the others did?"

"I didn't want to worry you. I thought if they believed me, you would never know about it. I didn't want to up-set you."

"Oh, Jody, you shouldn't worry about me. I don't need to be protected from your problems. I want to help you. I don't want you to end up in more trouble because of me. Now you're going to be kicked out of school."

"I don't care," he said vehemently.

"You don't care?" I said with surprise.

"I don't want to go there anymore."

"Why didn't you tell me this before?"

"I've tried to tell you. I told you I didn't like the upper school. They give you demerits for everything, even for throwing a snowball."

"But there have to be rules and regulations. Teenagers need discipline," I countered.

"Not that much. They treat you like prisoners."

"That's ridiculous, Jody. It's a very good school."

"See, that's what you always say. Every time I complain you say it's a very good school and that I'm lucky to be go-ing there."

"But you never came right out and said you didn't want to go there."

"Would it have made any difference if I had?" he asked.

"Probably," I said. "I would rather have told them you didn't want to go to school there anymore than to have them say you *can't* attend."

"No matter what the honor board says, I don't want to go back there next year, okay?"

"All right, Jody, but you'd better start thinking about where you do want to go."

I don't really believe kids should be allowed to change schools just because they don't like the rules or the teachers. I think they should be made to adjust. And maybe Jody was right—I wouldn't have considered letting him leave St. Paul's unless I was pushed into it. And perhaps, consciously or subconsciously, Jody participated in the incident at school and lied about it to push me into accepting a change of schools and to actually take the decision out of my hands.

The next afternoon Mr. Ordeman called me at the station to tell me the honor board had made its decision and to ask if Jody and I could meet with him at school the next morning.

"Certainly," I said. "We'll be there at eight-thirty if that's all right?"

"That's fine," he said and hung up.

He didn't say what the board's decision was, and I didn't ask. It no longer mattered.

Jody and I drove separate cars to St. Paul's that morning so that I could continue on to the station when the meeting was over and he could go back home. We met outside the mansion where the headmaster had his office. Jody looked the way I felt—nervous. I gave him a smile and said, "There's one thing I want you to do when this is over. I want you to shake hands with Mr. Ordeman and tell him you're sorry for the trouble you've caused."

Jody wrinkled his brow and shook his head in disapproval of that idea.

"Uh-uh," he mumbled.

"Yes," I said as we walked in.

Mr. Ordeman greeted us, then he sat down behind his big shiny desk. We sat in the two chairs in front of the desk, facing him. I felt as if we were sitting before a judge waiting to be sentenced. John Ordeman is a pleasant middle-aged man, balding, with glasses. He speaks in soft tones and rarely smiles. He is calm and cool, never appears to get excited, and never, ever is out of control. That is, I suppose, what it takes to be a headmaster of a boys' school. I wondered how many mothers and fathers had sat before him with their sons awaiting the bad news, as I was at that moment, how many times he had said, "This doesn't appear to be the right school for your boy."

"Jody, concerning the incident of the library cards found in the bottom of your locker," he began, "were you one of those who removed them from the backs of the library books?"

"Yes, sir," Jody said quietly.

"And the screws in the metal hardware on the library chairs and the wall fixtures—did you bring a screwdriver from home and take out the screws?"

"Yes, sir," he said again.

"I wish you had admitted that when the honor board questioned you. You told them you did not do those things. You lied. You know what that means?"

"Yes, sir."

"Mr. Ordeman," I broke in, "Jody has told me that he is not happy here at St. Paul's and no matter what the honor board has decided, he does not want to return next year."

Mr. Ordeman is a gentle, intuitive man who doesn't thrive on the pain or discomfort of others. He understood the purpose of my interruption, and as he continued he never actually said that the St. Paul's school was expelling Jody. Instead he talked about other school possibilities for Jody. And he said, "Jody, I hope you've learned from this experience. You're a very bright young man. Don't waste that gift."

"No, sir," Jody said, standing as Mr. Ordeman stood. He glanced at me with a look that asked, "Do I have to?"

I answered with a look that said, "Yes, you do."

Jody walked to the side of the desk and extended his hand to Mr. Ordeman. "I'm sorry for the trouble I've caused." His voice cracked and he was close to tears, but he did it. He looked back at me.

I smiled, trying to convey my love and approval. "You can go home," I said softly to my son. "I want to talk to Mr. Ordeman alone for a minute. I'll call you later."

When Jody had left and the door had closed behind him, my emotions, which I had been holding tightly in check, broke loose.

"He's a good boy," I said, sobbing. "I don't think he meant any real harm."

"I know he's a good boy," Mr. Ordeman said. "Maybe a change of school will be the best thing for him."

"I hope so. I love him so much."

Mr. Ordeman said he would make some calls for me

concerning other schools. I thanked him and left.

It was over and done with.

Things usually happen for the best, I thought, driving to work. Maybe a change of schools really will be good for Jody. But I was getting a little angry at what had just happened. Six years of my son's life had been spent at that school, not to mention thousands of dollars. What if Jody *had wanted* to stay there? He still would have been expelled for trying to spare me additional worry. Sure, he should have thought about that before he took part in the prank, but teenagers do dumb things sometimes. How can a school turn its back on a kid when he needs it most? Especially a school connected with the church? Where is its compassion and understanding? Is it the church's teaching that you throw a sinner out in the street? Or does it teach repentance, forgiveness, and compassion?

A year and a half before, Jody's father had committed suicide, and that school had promised to look after my son. They should have been aware that Jody might still be suffering from his father's death and needed their guidance and counseling more than ever. I know that rules are rules and that if you bend them for some, they may not work for others. But a troubled teenager should be given every chance to learn from a mistake—to learn *not* to give up or run away—and not be dismissed to start over in a new, alienating environment. And I think sometimes that means bending the rules. I was disappointed on that day more by the actions of a school I trusted than by those of my son. But maybe that was the reaction, or overreaction, of a mother who thought her son could do very little wrong.

That night after work Jack and Jody and I sat around

the kitchen table discussing what had happened and where Jody might go to school. Jody seemed relieved, more relaxed than he'd been in weeks.

"Do you want to go to Eddie's school?" I asked, referring to the high school to which Jody's friend went. "We'd have to pay a small tuition because it's located in Baltimore County and we live in Carroll County, but it would be nothing compared to what we were paying for private school."

"No, I don't want to go to public school," Jody said. "I wouldn't learn anything. I would be bored in that school. I already know more after the tenth grade than most seniors in public school."

"Lauren goes to that school," I teased, talking about the little pest who was now his heartthrob.

"No, Mom, forget it."

"Well, I'm glad you feel that way, Jody. I'm glad you don't want to coast for two years, have a good time, and graduate from any school just to be graduating."

"How do you feel about Poly?" Jack asked. "It's a public school, but it's as good as most private schools."

"I don't know," Jody said. "It sounds pretty good."

We had talked about Poly—Baltimore Polytechnic Institute. My father, my brother, and Jack had all gone there. The A course at Poly is an accelerated program for students planning to go into engineering or science in college and seemed tailor-made for Jody.

"You already have a lot of advanced math, maybe enough to go into the junior year without a great deal of tutoring," I pointed out.

"It's a four-year course, and you'd be going in halfway through, but perhaps with some classes this summer, you could make it," Jack said.

"It would certainly be worth a try," I said, "and you sure wouldn't be wasting the next two years."

"Of course you could always do what I did and take the B course, or even the general course," Jack said.

"I wouldn't want to do that," Jody said shyly.

"I didn't think you would," Jack said with a smile.

"Then it's settled. I'll call Poly tomorrow and I'll get an application. We'll go in for an interview and see what happens. Okay?"

"Okay," said Jody as if he had just been relieved of some very heavy burden. "I'm going out and ride my motorcycle until dinner's ready, okay?"

"Okay," I said, "but don't be long. Dinner will be ready in about twenty minutes."

I watched him through the kitchen window as he walked toward the motorcycle shed with his helmet in his hand. I smiled and turned to face Jack, who was now standing behind me.

"Thank you," I said as I put my arms around this man whom I loved so much and even more at that moment. "Thank you for helping Jody with this problem."

"I didn't do anything," Jack said.

"You were here. You made him feel better by being here."

"I wanted to hug him," Jack confessed. "Even though he's sixteen and not my son, I wanted to reach out and put my arms around him."

"I wish you had," I said as I tightened my arms around him and put my head on his shoulder.

"So do I," he said with regret.

CHAPTER 7
A BRIGHT FUTURE
AUGUST 1976

HE wind was blowing my hair across my face as I stood on the sun deck looking out across the almost deserted beach. A lone fisherman was standing at the water's edge challenging the tide. I listened to the roar of the waves as the ocean moved closer to our house. I loved the sea, the sound, and that special salty smell, free of big city pollution.

I felt like a girl again when I stood watching the waves or walking on the beach. I loved being back by the ocean. It wasn't really our house, we were renting it. But it was ours for two weeks—two glorious weeks. The whole family was together: Marjorie, her boy friend—also named Jody—O'Donnell, Jody White—as we were now calling him to differentiate between the two Jodys—Jack, and Christopher. Jody White's friends would be in and out, and Jack's nephew Doug would be staying for a while. Even Marjorie's dog, Jackson, a Doberman pinscher, was with us. I couldn't remember ever being happier. I could hear the sound of those I loved inside in the living room, laughing and talking. The sound of peace and solitude in front of me washed in with each wave. Tears of joy began to well up and fill my eyes.

We'd all been through a lot, but our lives seemed to be coming together now. It had been almost two years since John's suicide. The kids were doing pretty well, I thought. They seemed happy and active and involved with their friends. I was pleased with the adjustments they had apparently made. If there were problems at that point, they were hiding them from me. Jack and I appeared to have overcome the legacy of guilt and incrimination that John had left us. There were many problems for the two of us to deal with as I tried to come to terms with my feelings of love for Jack and my recurring self-hatred, the feeling that I had no right to love or be loved, that I wasn't worthy of love. After all, I had caused a man to kill himself.

There were times when I pulled away from Jack completely, showing him that I was unreliable and unworthy of his love and faithfulness and that he would be better off without me. But he wouldn't accept any of it, and through his patience, persistence, and perceptions he made me see that we did have a right to *our* love and happiness. The path to that discovery wasn't always pleasant. We had many heated arguments as he forced me to face what I was doing and why.

John and I had never argued. We had never exchanged harsh words or shouted at each other. All the pain and problems were kept beneath the surface. The first time Jack raised his voice to me I was stunned. I said, "No man has ever shouted at me—not my father and not my husband—and I'm certainly not going to take it from you." Jack wasn't ready to let me off the hook with that cop-out.

He forced me to come forth with my real feelings and to challenge him—which I started doing, and not always in a ladylike way.

The sharp words we spoke were like a surgeon's knife removing a cancer that could have destroyed us. Once the disease was removed, we healed and our love grew strong. We had become more sure of each other, and Jack had asked me to marry him. We decided that we wouldn't get married right away, but in about a year. We saw no reason to rush things. I still needed time to adjust to the idea of once again being someone's wife, and Jack wanted to be as sure as he could that our marriage wouldn't end up like his other two—in divorce. Jack had begun to wonder if anyone could live with him and his idiosyncrasies. But we felt confident that our love would only get stronger as the months passed, so we became engaged.

When you're in the public eye, engagements don't go by with a simple announcement in the social pages of the newspapers. I smiled to myself as I thought about the attention our engagement had gotten from other members of the Baltimore media. Even TV news people on the other stations announced that we were planning to be married.

Of course I told the children before anyone else. Jody was the first one I talked to about our marriage plans. I was concerned about how he would react. He liked Jack and they got along well, but they weren't really close. Jody listened carefully and with interest when Jack talked about news and current events, when he told the interesting or funny tidbits he'd picked up in the numerous papers and magazines he read every day. And Jack listened intently when Jody spoke about math problems or a complicated puzzle he'd solved in a matter of minutes when no one else in the family or classroom had been able to. Jack even listened when Jody talked about his motorcycle racing, even though that wasn't a prime interest for Jack. Each had his own areas of expertise and his own time and territory when it came to me, so I wasn't sure how Jody would react when I told him Jack would be crossing over that imaginary, unspoken line to become my husband and his stepfather.

Jody and I were standing in the kitchen. I was fixing him something to eat and he was getting a soft drink from the refrigerator.

"I've got some news for you," I said, choosing each word carefully. "Good news, I think. Jack and I have decided to get married."

Jody wheeled around to face me. He hadn't had time to camouflage his feelings. His face was washed with shock and surprise.

"How come?" he asked bluntly.

"Well, we love each other—you know that. He thinks the world of you and the girls, and I'm fond of Christopher. And you know Christopher thinks you're the most marvelous thing since Superman. You're his hero. We think that we'll make a good family. What do you think?"

"I don't care," he mumbled, his emotions now neatly under control.

"What do you mean, you don't care? Do you think it's a good idea?" I asked gently.

"I don't know. It doesn't matter to me." He turned around to continue what he had been doing before I'd startled him with the news. I got the message that it did matter to Jody if I got married, but instead of putting my arms around him and telling him how much I loved him and that no one could ever take his place in my affections, I tried to reassure him by backing off a bit.

"We won't be getting married right away, probably not for a year or so."

"It doesn't matter," he repeated. I let it drop, and as the weeks passed he seemed to become accustomed to the idea.

Marjorie and O'Donnell were delighted with the news. Both the girls loved Jack's sense of humor and his corny jokes. He made them laugh, and it was so good to hear that laughter. Jody loved and respected his sisters and would go along with what either or both of them wanted. I think when he saw that they were pleased about the marriage he thought that maybe it would be okay. I don't think he was afraid that Jack would be a bossy stepfather and try to push him around, but he probably thought that I would have less time for him.

I should have asked, so that I could have really reassured him. But I didn't.

"Hi, you look beautiful standing there," Jack said as he walked up behind me and put his arm around my waist. "I love you," he whispered.

"I love you too, more than I could ever tell you. I'm so happy."

"So am I," he confessed. "I'm glad we're getting married."

"Are you?" I questioned.

"Yes, I am," he said, reassuring me.

"I'm so afraid you'll feel trapped, feel afraid that this marriage won't work any better than your others."

"Don't worry about it," he said. "Everything will be fine."

"Dad," came a little voice from the other side of the sliding screen door. We turned to see Christopher pressing his face against the screen, peering out at us. "Dad, Jody says he can beat you at wrestling. He can't, can he, Dad?"

"Probably," said Jack. "He's a lot younger and stronger. Remember, Christopher, he rides motorcycles."

"Well, he can't outwrestle me," I said in a challenging but kidding way as I walked off the deck and back into the house.

"You want to bet?" said Jody equally as challenging, with a big smile on his face.

"Sure," I said. "I've got a brand new two-dollar bill hot off the presses that says I can pin you and probably without much effort."

"Oh, yeah? You're on," he said, laughing with delight. We loved to wrestle and roughhouse. There was no way I could beat Jody at wrestling, but it was fun to try. I am strong, so I could give him a run for his money—or should I say my money?

I got him almost pinned, and then he broke loose. We twisted and strained and pulled and tugged and, most important, we laughed. Eventually I ended up flat on the floor, out of breath, with my shoulders pinned down, admitting I had been beaten but vowing to reverse the outcome the next time. I got up and got the two-dollar bill out of my wallet.

"You'd better save that. You may not ever get another one. They may stop printing them, and you may stop beating me."

"No way, Mom—you're weak, face it. You're getting old. Remember, you're thirty-seven now," Jody kidded.

"And I'm sure you won't let me forget it."

"Jack," I said, "I think we ought to have some champagne before dinner. Let's celebrate our first night in Ocean City."

The cork was popped, glasses filled.

"A toast," said Marjorie. "A toast to Jack." She paused, looked at me, then looked back into the face of the man she might have resented, might even have blamed for contributing to her father's suicide. "Thank you for making my mother so happy."

Tears sprang into our eyes as we felt the emotional depth of what Marjorie had said and realized the meaning behind the words she spoke. She was absolving Jack and me of all blame for her father's death. She had suffered much pain, and she missed her dad a great deal, but she did not want us to feel guilty and she did not resent our happiness. O'Donnell and Jody stood smiling in agreement. Jack put his arms around Marjorie.

"I hope I'll always be able to make your mother happy."

I hugged them both, then O'Donnell, Jody, and Christopher. We were already a family, I thought.

I went to the kitchen to put dinner on the table. It would be a wonderful two weeks, I thought again, and I smiled; it had already been a very good summer.

Jody had been accepted at Poly. The marks on his tests were very high. He did have to go to summer school to take a few advanced courses in math, which he hadn't gotten at St. Paul's, such as trigonometry.

Summer school was a breeze for Jody. He got the top marks in his class, and he was now ready to begin regular classes in the fall. He was educationally prepared, and he was looking forward to a new beginning in a new school. Of course he was also a bit apprehensive. He was nervous about going to such a big school with several thousand students. It was a big change from the small private school that had only several hundred. Just finding his way around the building would be a challenge, and making friends for someone as shy as Jody would be difficult. But he had attended summer school there, so he was acquainted with the layout of the school. I was probably more apprehensive about what he faced than he was. It was always that way. I took on what I felt were his concerns or worries or pain and made them mine. Perhaps I thought I could take those uncomfortable feelings away from him and he wouldn't have to suffer. But of course what happened was that we both suffered.

How much better it would have been if I had helped him face his insecurities, deal with them, and conquer them. How much better if we had talked about those feelings before they caused either of us real concern. How much better off we both would have been. But I didn't talk. I just felt. When he was shaky, so was I. When he felt joy, it was reflected in my mood. (He has my sensitivity, I told myself—it can be a blessing or it can be a curse, but we share it.)

The closeness hurt at times, but it also brought great moments of happiness, such as the time of my last birthday. It was a couple of weeks before we went to Ocean City, August 4, my thirty-seventh birthday. I was feeling a little old and a lot forgotten as I left the station that night after getting off the air. No one had suggested any kind of birthday celebration, neither the kids nor Jack. As a matter of fact, no one had even mentioned my birthday, and since I don't like to remind people to remember me, I hadn't said anything.

Driving home, I was feeling really sorry for myself, thinking about how I always made a big deal about their birthdays. I was trying to reverse my self-centered thinking as I pulled into the driveway, reminding myself that I got as much out of "the doing" as they got out of "the receiving." I was trying, but I wasn't succeeding as I walked into the very quiet house. Then I saw the dining room, and everything changed. Not only was the table set for dinner, there were bright balloons, and in the center of the table was a vase filled with black-eyed Susans, my favorite flower. As I stood there taking in the warmth and color of the room and the moment, the children came out of the kitchen.

"Happy birthday, Mom. Surprise!"

"You guys are too much. I thought everyone had forgotten my birthday. This is really nice. It really is!!"

"That's what we wanted you to think," said Marjorie. "Otherwise we couldn't surprise you."

"I guess Jack was in on this little secret?" I asked.

"Yep. I called him and told him not to say a word. He'll be here soon," Marjorie announced, pleased with herself and her plans.

"O'Donnell's doing the cooking," she went on, "because I knew you wouldn't want to eat dinner if I did it."

"That's true," I said, smiling at Marjorie's acknowledgment of her lack of talent in the kitchen.

"And she baked a cake," Marjorie went on.

"Who picked the flowers?" I asked.

"Jody," Marjorie said.

I was pretty sure he had before I asked the question, but I thought maybe at age sixteen, Jody had outgrown such acts of sentiment, at least toward his mother. I was glad he hadn't. I looked at my son, who appeared embarrassed at being caught in an act of caring but pleased that I was pleased.

"Thank you. I love them. They're beautiful. Where did you find so many? I didn't think there were that many left around here."

"I found them on the other side of the hillside pasture." I looked at the bright yellow flowers with the dark-brown centers and remembered all the other times Jody had brought me black-eyed Susans.

When he was just a little boy we would go for walks together and he would pick the flowers because they were bright and stood out in the green fields. He would run back to me each time he pulled one. His short, chubby little legs stumbled across the rough pastureland and a smile of accomplishment stretched across his face.

"I ot other un, ommy," his little voice would call out as he got near. With his arm extended, he carried the flower like an olympic torch, high and triumphantly.

I would take each one he gave me and add it to the others he'd brought before.

"Thank you," I would say. "Thank you for this beautiful flower. It's my very favorite one. This is more beautiful than all the rest." The next and the next was the most beautiful. He always found one a little more special than the one before. It was a game we played, and it kept him looking for black-eyed Susans. When we got home I would put them in a vase on the kitchen table. Jody saw how these wild flowers pleased me, so when he got a little older and ventured out on his own, he continued to come home occasionally with a fistful of flowers to brighten my day.

When I first decided that my troubled marriage was more than I could tolerate and felt I was losing control of myself and my life, I was discussing it with John on the back lawn. I told him I had gotten an apartment and would be moving out. At that point Jody drove up on his minibike with a bunch of black-eyed Susans crushed between his hand and the throttle of the motorcycle. He had picked them in a field where he had been riding and had driven back to give them to me. The stems were broken and bent, and when Jody held the flowers out to me, they fell limp, like a bunch of cooked spaghetti. I smiled, even laughed a little, at the sight of those forlorn flowers. But Jody had been thinking of me, and he had stopped what he was doing to pick them and bring them back to me. I was touched.

"Thank you, they're beautiful," I said. "I'll put them in water. They'll come back."

Having delivered the flowers, Jody roared off on his motorcycle, heading back to the field to continue his ride. When he was gone, John spoke.

"If you do what you say you're going to do and move out—leave me and the children—not only will Jody never bring you any more black-eyed Susans, he'll never want to see you or speak to you again."

I went inside, picked up the phone, and canceled the rental of the apartment. The limp bunch of flowers and the thought that I might never get such a wonderful gift again because I might lose the love of my son kept me at home in an agonizing situation for six more months. When I finally realized I had to leave to maintain my sanity, I decided I would have to trust the depth of my son's love for me and hope it could endure my absence. It did. Obviously, it did, I thought, as my vision once again focused on the black-eyed Susans in the center of my dining room table.

"Happy birthday," Jack said as he walked into the dining room. "Surprise!"

"It is a happy birthday, and it has certainly been a surprise," I said. "You shouldn't keep secrets from me," I scolded.

"Your children wanted to surprise you. Did you want me to spoil that for them?"

"No, I guess not. Look at the flowers Jody picked for me," I said, my voice quavering as I tried not to cry.

"That's nice," he said as he put his arms around me and hugged me. "You should be very proud of your children and very pleased that they care about you enough to do something like this."

"I am. Believe me, I am."

At one point during dinner, when I was in the kitchen with Marjorie and O'Donnell, Jack said to Jody, "Jody, that was really wonderful, the flowers and the dinner. You and your sisters have made your mother very happy. She'll never forget this night."

Jody nodded and smiled shyly. He was pleased with what Jack had said, but his shyness kept him from speaking in response.

Thinking about that as I stood in the kitchen of the Ocean City beach house, I realized that Jack didn't have to tell Jody he had pleased me. Jody knew he had pleased me, because he had been doing it all his life.

"Hi, Mom, how're you doing?"

I swung around to see Jody's friends Tommy, Eddie, and Doug standing in the doorway.

"Hi, guys."

"Boy, did you get a lot of sun today," Tommy observed. "You look gorgeous, though—better than anything I've seen down on the boardwalk."

Some teenagers certainly aren't shy, I thought.

"Your timing is perfect. Dinner is just about ready. How *did* you know?" I kidded them.

"Well, actually we've been waiting outside for an hour, and when I saw you through the window putting the food on the table, I said, 'Let's go—it's time for chow,'" Tommy said, continuing to kid with me. Tommy was glib, self-assured, the complete opposite of Jody. He was a little younger than the other boys, but he acted much older. Tommy was not yet sixteen; he didn't have his driver's license, but that didn't slow down his social life one bit. He dated older girls, who did the driving. They would pick him up after school, at home, at a motorcycle race, anywhere at all. He was in great demand, and I hardly ever saw him with the same girl twice. Tommy, I feared, was setting a standard of living that the other kids, including Jody, would like to achieve.

"Where's Jody?" Eddie asked.

"He's upstairs showering and changing his clothes, getting ready for a big night on the boardwalk."

"You mean a big night with Lauren, don't you?"

Eddie's words stopped me cold.

"I didn't know Lauren was down here," I said as calmly and coolly as I could, trying to be nonchalant and seem just mildly interested to hear that my son's girl friend was also in Ocean City—something Jody had neglected to tell me.

"If Jody went to the moon, Lauren would find a way to get there also," Tommy commented. "Is it okay if we go upstairs to Jody's room?"

"Sure, it's the room in the back with all the bunk beds— plenty of room for you guys if you want to spend the night."

"Thanks, but I think we're going to camp out at Eddie's place or maybe sleep on the beach."

"Hey, Jody," Tommy called out as they all traipsed up the stairs. "Make sure you use lots of after-shave lotion. I hear Lauren loves after-shave lotion."

"Would you also tell him to hurry up? Dinner is almost ready," I called out after them. Lauren, I thought, does have a way of showing up everywhere.

After dinner Jody told me as he and the boys left the house that he would be staying at Eddie's house or sleeping on the beach. I reminded them that sleeping on the beach was against the law and that Eddie's parents might not be so happy about everyone's descending on them.

"Oh, they don't care. They like having us around."

"Well, so do I, and we have that great big room upstairs with all those beds. I'll leave the door open just in case you change your mind." He didn't change his mind, and the next day as I sat out on the beach soaking up the late morning sun, I was wishing he had. I wasn't ready to give up my son and turn him over to his friends for the entire vacation.

Jack and I had rented this particular beach house because it had the large upstairs dormitory-type room that would provide plenty of space for Jody and his friends. We wanted them all to feel welcome. It was the part of the vacation I'd been looking forward to most—having Jody and the boys around, having two weeks when I didn't need to go anywhere or do anything but spend time with my family.

I realized that it was normal for teenagers of sixteen and seventeen to be off and running to congregate on common ground. I had just hoped that our place would be the hangout.

I looked out across the sand and watched a little boy with light blond hair playing at the water's edge. He kept running back to his mother, who was sitting in a beach chair reading. He wanted her to come with him to look at something in the water. She must have been saying, "Not right now—in a little while." He would run back and stare into the water by himself. I wondered if she realized that in a little while there would be no little boy, that he'd be grown up, and that it would be she who would be alone looking at the ocean. I hadn't realized how fast *my* little boy would grow beyond my reach. I guess no parent does. Now I didn't even know where he was or what he was doing. I wondered what was going on in his life that I didn't know about.

I lay back on my towel, closed my eyes, and let the warmth of the sun take me back to other summers when Jody wanted to be with his mother more than he wanted to be with anyone else, when I knew where he was every minute. I smiled as I thought about the times in Cape May, New Jersey, when Jody and I would sneak off before breakfast and bicycle to the south end of the beach where the fishermen went out before sunrise to try their luck from the stone jetties. There was a little restaurant there, and sometimes we'd get scrambled eggs or pancakes and watch the sun come up over the ocean. Then we'd race our bicycles back down the beach road, up onto the boardwalk, and when we got back to my inlaws' house, we would tell no one that we had eaten breakfast. It was our secret.

I wish I had my little boy back, I thought, just for a day, so I could spend some time with him on the beach to fly a kite or play in the waves or look for the prettiest seashell in the whole world. Seashells are like black-eyed Susans. Each one we found was more beautiful than the last. It was so simple then when love *was* enough.

A shadow crossed my face, and I opened my eyes to see what clouds had moved in to block the sun, and there they were. The four boys stood over me like giants about to squash a helpless little sand crab. I sat up with a start.

"Where did you all come from? Where have you been? When did you get here?"

"We walked up the beach from One Hundred Thirtieth Street," Jody said. "We've been water-skiing with Eddie's father. We just got here and we're starved."

"Good," I said as I stood up. "I'll whip up some Egg McWhites in no time flat. Now, I have regular Egg Mc-Whites, Beachcomber McWhites, or Beachbum McWhites."

"What are the last two?" Jody asked, suspicious of my new creations.

"Beachcomber McWhites are scrambled eggs with crab on an English muffin. Beachbums are eggs, hamburgers, cheese, lettuce, and tomatoes on an English muffin."

"I'll have a Beachbum," said Jody.

"You are hungry, aren't you? How about you guys?"

"I'll have the same."

"Me too."

"I'll have one also."

"Okay, four Beachbums for my four beachbums. Come on up on the deck, sit down and relax, and I'll get you some orange juice."

Jack was sitting on the couch reading the paper as I walked through the living room on my way to the kitchen.

"The boys are back. I'm going to fix them something to eat, then let's go to the water slide or race go-carts or something."

"Fine," said Jack. "We'll all go. I think Christopher would love to do that."

We had a wonderful time. The teenage boys were acting like carefree kids again, laughing and carrying on as they came flying down the watery shoot. I loved to see them play with such abandon. They looked like young colts with long gangly legs and free-flowing manes, showing off for me and each other.

Jody's hair was longer than I liked it but not as long as some of his friends' hair. It was the style of that hippie era, a style that I and most parents hated. While Jody was at St. Paul's School he was required to keep his hair above his shirt collar, but now he had let it grow a little longer. Jody knew I preferred his hair cut short, so he compromised—just over the ears and a little longer in back. He kept it washed and neat; I didn't have any real problem with that. He had never rebelled, like some kids, refusing to get a haircut and growing it shoulder length or longer. I knew Jody wasn't trying to make a statement with his hair, he was just going along with the other kids and the style of the seventies. It didn't bother me *that* much. And on that particular afternoon I had no worries at all. The kids were with me having fun, and so was I. I joined them on the slide. I loved being one of the guys. And Jody always seemed pleased and proud to have me join in. But more important than being part of the gang or doing things other mothers wouldn't, I loved sharing these times with Jody. And it was obvious he also enjoyed my companionship in activities like these. He'd coax me on and laugh at my mistakes or silliness and cheer my triumphs. Jody was my greatest audience, and I was his.

It also pleased me to watch the boys take little Christopher down the slide for the first time—slow and easy, so he wouldn't be frightened.

Such gentle teenagers, I thought. So rough with each

other, so soft and kind with a child. Tough riding their motorcycles, tender with a little boy on a water slide. They'll make good fathers, I thought with pride and pleasure. The idea of Jody's child, my grandchild, was a reassuring one, a promise that the warmth I was experiencing at that moment would recur from time to time throughout my life. Someday I would see Jody teaching his own child the fun of trying new experiences.

We dried off and moved on from the water slide to the go-carts. All of us were speeding around the track, ducking and dodging and maneuvering. The big kids used their moto-cross abilities to cut and corner and, for the most part, stay out in front, while I called on my competitive nature to try as hard as I could to keep up with them. Jack and Christopher, together in one cart, took it easy. We all zoomed around them and past them, yelling and laughing as we flew by. It was wonderful. I wished that every day of our vacation could be like that day.

But Jody continued to spend only a part of his days with us, usually mealtimes, and the rest of the time, including nights, he spent with his friends. He never brought Lauren back to our house, even though I suggested that he should. For some reason he was keeping that part of his life separate from his family life. I was bothered by all of this. Finally, after almost a week of his sleeping away from home, I insisted that he come back to our house to spend the night. I didn't know what he was doing or what kind of trouble he might be getting into—having sex with Lauren or, what I feared more than anything, taking drugs.

I knew the family with whom he was staying; the parents were wonderful but permissive, as many of us were at that time. Back then parents didn't talk to other parents about potential problems. We didn't band together to provide strength for one another and protection for our kids. Jody might have been staying out all night and they wouldn't have told me. They might have thought I didn't care, because I'd never told them otherwise. I decided I wanted Jody with us where I could keep an eye on him.

"I don't care if it's more fun to stay with Eddie," I told him. "I don't care if you feel confined and restricted with us and don't like having to come in earlier here. You have a family and a place to stay, and I want you back here every night. You can bring your friends back with you, but I want you here at night. Is that clear?" I asked.

"Yes," Jody said, not happy about my demand but not unhappy enough to dispute it.

It may have put a damper on his teenage fun and newly found freedom at the beach, but he obeyed my order and started coming home about two o'clock each morning, which I accepted because I didn't want to be too much of a killjoy. I wondered, though, why Jody preferred to stay elsewhere, why he felt more comfortable at someone else's house. I wondered if he was uncomfortable with Jack and me sleeping together, unmarried. I wondered if he had grown jealous of little Christopher and the attention I gave him. There was one day on the beach that made me think that this might be the case. It was a gray day, when the surf seemed angry at the absence of sun and people. The waves pounded the white sandy shoreline with a vengeance. But Jody and his buddies had decided they would take on the ocean in spite of the size and roughness of the waves.

Christopher and I stood at the edge of the water watching them body-surf. I held his hand as I spoke to him and tried to calm the natural fears of this little boy. When I looked up, Jody was moving himself into position to catch a wave. The water swelled to at least nine feet. It was a giant wave, and Jody would either get a sensational ride or be twisted like a pretzel. I held my breath and said a quick prayer, as I did each time he came off the starting line at a motorcycle race. "Oh, God, please let him be all right and get through this safely."

The wall of water curled over him and crashed down with tremendous force. But as the wave rolled toward us, Jody's head was out in front. The rest of his body, held rigidly afloat like a piece of driftwood, was being carried along with the incredible power of the churning water. The closer to shore the wave came, the smaller it got, until at last it was reduced to a mere line of foam floating on top of the shallow water.

"Look, Christopher," I said, pointing to the sudsy remainder of something that just minutes ago was big and frightening. "Look at the wave now. It couldn't hurt a flea."

Jody was walking toward us. He was out of breath, but he was exhilarated.

"That was some ride," I said. "I thought you were a goner."

"So did I," he confessed, smiling at me.

But as his gaze dropped to little Christopher clinging to my hand the smile disappeared, and he turned back toward his friends, who were sitting on the beach resting.

"Did you see that one I just came in on?" he called out as he walked to join them. I felt guilty. Did he think Christopher could replace him in my feelings?

Did Jody feel that because I no longer took his hand in mine I had stopped caring about his safety, his life? Had we, in fact, lost touch with each other? After all, I didn't know what was going on in his life right then. Was he spending the majority of his time, days and nights, with his friends because I didn't provide him with enough love and understanding to make him feel secure? Was he allowing himself to be carried along with the crowd, just as he had been carried in by the wave, because that was the strongest force in his life at the moment, the one providing the biggest thrill and the most security? Did I give him a good reason to resist the joyride? Had I told him about the dangers that exist in the teenage trip into adulthood?

I hadn't even warned him that people break their necks riding waves, that dozens of people each year end up being paralyzed for the rest of their lives from surf-riding. Why was I taking chances with the physical and emotional health of my son? Why did I continue to believe that everything would turn out all right? Why didn't I realize that he needed my guidance and my affection? Kids don't outgrow the need to be hugged and touched. They need physical contact. They need to have someone hold their hands. You don't outgrow that need when you become a teenager. It grows with you and, perhaps, it becomes even more important that the need be met.

Jody must have felt displaced. But I couldn't see it. In my mind and in my heart no one was more important to me than my son. But he obviously didn't know it, and my simply wanting him to understand it didn't make it happen.

I'm going to have a good talk with Jody, I thought, as I led Christopher back across the sand to the beach house, where Jack sat watching from the sun deck. "I think I'll do a little wave-riding with the boys," I said as I delivered Christopher to his father's side.

"It's dangerous out there today, Susan. Don't be crazy," Jack warned.

"I'm strong and I'm a good swimmer—you know that—and I'll be careful."

"You've never been careful in your life, and you're no match for those waves."

"I'll be all right. It looks like fun," I said as I walked down the steps and across the sand to where the boys sat.

I was going to reassure my son of my love and affection in the way I knew best, the only way I could do it comfortably, the way my father had shown me he cared. I was going to join the kids in what they were doing. I was going to be his friend, one of the guys.

"Okay, you guys, you've rested long enough. Let's show this ocean who's boss."

"All right, Mom's going in and ride the waves," Eddie exclaimed. Jody smiled, got up, and we ran into the surf, side by side.

I've got to have that talk, I thought, someday real soon, so he knows how I feel.

We dove into the first wave and came up on the other side.

"I'll beat you to the big breakers," I called out as I started to swim. Someday real soon, I thought.

CHAPTER 8

THE FUTURE DIMS
FEBRUARY 1977

*W*HEN the talk finally came, it was six months later. Even then I was forced into it, and it didn't involve the questions that had been on my mind before. It was precipitated by something I honestly didn't think I would have to face—Jody's use of drugs. We parents have a great way of kidding ourselves about our children. We believe what we want to believe and deny what we don't want to face.

The revelation about Jody came from his sister after Jody had been in an auto accident while driving her car. He, fortunately, was not hurt. The car had been repaired, and I was at the station talking about it on the phone with O'Donnell. O'Donnell was home from college for the semester break.

"You know I don't mind Jody driving the car, Mom. It's only that I don't like him driving in the condition he's in sometimes. He's just going to wreck it again."

The words stunned me.

"Do you mean what I think you mean? That your brother uses drugs, that Jody smokes marijuana?"

"Yes, Mother—he's been doing it for some time."

I was shocked. I didn't want to believe it, but I knew my daughter wouldn't lie to me. I didn't know what to do or what to say.

He had promised me he wouldn't smoke pot. I just didn't believe Jody would go along with the crowd. I believed he would keep his word to me, no matter what. Maybe I was putting too much reliance on his self-control. I suppose there was too little guidance from me and too much pressure from his friends. My shock turned to anger. How could he do this to me? How could he deceive me, go against his word, break the trust I had in him?

"Why didn't you tell me this before?" I questioned O'Donnell.

"I didn't want to be the one to tell on him. But I just don't like him driving my car when he's smoking."

"Is Jody home now?"

"Yes."

"Let me talk to him," I demanded.

"Hello," Jody said as he picked up the phone.

"Jody, O'Donnell has just told me that you smoke pot. I cannot begin to tell you how upset and disappointed I am. I don't want you to go anywhere tonight. I don't care if it's Friday night and I don't care if you have made plans. First thing tomorrow morning we are going to have a discussion about this. Is that understood?"

"Yes," he said meekly without a word of protest.

"You and O'Donnell, and I'm going to ask Jack to be there also. I'll see you later, okay?"

"Okay."

I hung up the phone. I was panicking, just as I had

when I found out Marjorie had been smoking pot. What could I possibly say to make an impression on my son? He already knew I was against pot smoking and still he was doing it.

That evening I sat on the carpet in Jack's living room. A plateful of Stouffer's stuffed pasta, spinach from a hot plastic bag, and Jack's own fresh salad were on the coffee table between us. Over what had become my favorite dinner—since I didn't have to cook it—I told him about my new problem with Jody.

"I guess I should have gone home tonight and faced this problem with him right away. But I don't know what to say, what to do. I just want it to go away. I don't want my child involved with this stuff, but how do I order him to stop doing it without having him hate me, without having him rebel?"

I was such an escape artist. I would do anything to avoid confronting an uncomfortable problem. If I had faced all the previous problems, discussed them with the right person, and done something to correct them, I might not have been in that predicament at that moment.

"I don't know," Jack answered. "We'll just have to wait until tomorrow and see what Jody says."

"I don't even know anything about pot. I don't know if it's really bad for you or safer than booze, as so many say."

"We all know people who use pot," Jack was saying. "I've tried it a few times. It slows everything down, and I felt as if I were walking on cotton. I sure wouldn't want to drive in that condition."

"Well, I've never tried it, and I don't want to, and I don't want my son smoking it. I just wish I knew what to say to stop him."

"Don't get yourself all upset. Let's wait and see how it

goes tomorrow," Jack said. He took my hand in his, leaned across the table, and kissed me.

The next morning I was in my kitchen fixing coffee by seven-thirty. I normally would sleep until at least nine on a Saturday, but not this Saturday. I had been awake since six, lying in bed thinking.

Jack had driven home with me so he would be at the house for the early-morning discussion. Our sleeping together was nothing new, and the children seemed to accept it. But I felt much better when I spent the night at Jack's apartment on the few occasions when Jody was sleeping over at a friend's house. When we slept at my house, with the children there, somehow I felt as if I were doing something wrong. I was not happy about the example we were setting, even though living together had become socially acceptable.

But I either had to deal with my guilt feelings or not spend as much time with Jack, because neither of us was really ready to try another marriage, not just yet. We had even called off our engagement, feeling our wedding plans had been premature. Jack was nervous; he was afraid of another failure. I was afraid of belonging to another man. Neither of us wanted to give up our independence, and we weren't sure that our personal freedom could be maintained if we got married. I felt that what we were doing was right for us at the time, but I wasn't sure it was right for my children or for Jack's son. On the other hand, the security of marriage and one home would be much better for them. And so I battled with my conscience constantly. Not that it did any good or brought about any changes.

Jack was the first one to join me in the kitchen. I poured him a glass of orange juice and a cup of coffee.

"How do you feel?" he asked.

"Not very good," I answered. "I didn't sleep very well, and I feel really shaky. But I'll be all right. Thank you for being here," I said as I put my arms around him. "I love you. I don't know what I'd do without you."

"I love you too," he said as he folded his arms around me and held me tight. "If you want me here, I'll always be here. I don't know what good I'll be, but I'm here."

The strength from his arms seemed to pass into my body, calming the jittery sensation in the pit of my stomach and easing the weakness in my legs. My neck went limp as I rested my head on his shoulder, and I allowed him to carry the weight of my worry for a few minutes.

"Just having you here helps—believe me, it does."

I felt a lump forming in my throat and tears coming to my eyes. No, I can't give in to emotion, I thought, not now. I've got to be strong enough to do Jody some good. I straightened up, pulled away from Jack's support, and turned to the stove to fix some bacon and eggs.

I could hear someone coming downstairs, and I turned around as O'Donnell came through the kitchen door.

"Good morning," I said, "and how are you today?"

"Okay."

"Would you like some breakfast?"

"I'll get it," she answered as she went to the refrigerator and took out the bottle of orange juice and a couple of English muffins.

She sat across from Jack at the round oak table at the end of the kitchen. He asked about school, and she answered, making polite conversation. Everyone was avoiding the subject we were gathering to talk about. I poured a cup of coffee and sat in the chair next to Jack, also facing O'Donnell. A few minutes later Jody walked into the room. We all turned in his direction. He was wearing dungarees and his favorite red plaid flannel shirt. His hair was getting long again, but this was no time to talk about getting it cut, I thought. The straggly dark mustache of a teenage boy who has never shaved his upper lip also bothered me, but I wouldn't bring that up today either. Underneath the hair is my handsome son, I thought. Why does he want to look like that? I guess all Jack sees is an unkempt kid who we now find out is a pothead.

For the first time I was seeing my son through the eyes of someone else. And I didn't like what I saw. I wanted to reject the image. My Jody looked like a druggie.

The thought made me want to jump to Jody's defense before we had even started the conversation. I couldn't stand the thought that Jack or anyone else didn't see Jody as I saw him—a good, sensitive, caring child, intelligent and knowledgeable about many things, capable, physically and mentally, a devoted son and a loving brother, fun to be with, easygoing and never, ever difficult.

As he stood there facing us he looked like a convicted man standing before the judge and jury, waiting to hear the sentence. My heart went out to him. I wanted to protect him, not condemn him.

"Sit down, Jody. I'll get you some breakfast."

"I'm not hungry," he said as he sat down.

"You have to eat something."

"I don't want anything, Mom."

"Well, have some orange juice anyway," I said as I put the glass of juice on the table in front of him. "You have to have something in your stomach."

He picked up the glass and drank the orange juice. I sat next to him. There was silence as we all waited for someone to begin. It was up to me, I thought. I had ordered this meeting. I looked at Jody.

"How long have you been smoking marijuana?"

He looked down at the table. "Since last May," he mumbled.

"Since last May!" I said, raising my voice in shock.

He looked up to face me again. "Yeah, since last May."

"How can that be? How could you be using pot all that time without my knowing it?"

" 'Cause I don't get out of control. I don't stagger around or get so wasted I pass out. Sometimes I get high here at home, and you've never noticed because I don't change that much."

"Why, Jody? Why do you do it?"

"It makes me feel better, and I need it to study."

"What? How can you study on that stuff?"

"It calms me down. I need it to be able to do three straight hours of homework. I wouldn't be able to do as well at Poly without it."

"Then you're in the wrong school. You shouldn't have to take drugs to do schoolwork."

"I like Poly. I want to go there."

"I can't believe you need pot to study. I just can't believe it. If you do well on that stuff, think what you could do without it. Think what you could do if you were clear-headed."

"I wouldn't be able to concentrate for long periods of time without it."

I just sat there shaking my head. I couldn't believe what I was hearing. I couldn't believe what my son was saying to me.

"It's wrong for you, Jody. You have a brilliant mind. I don't want to see you mess it up with drugs. Where do you get the stuff?"

"Aw, Mom, you can get pot anywhere."

"At Poly?"

"Yeah, but not just at Poly. I got it at St. Paul's too when I was there."

I shook my head some more. Marijuana had obviously won over my child, and I didn't know what to do or say to get him back.

"How about your friends? Do they smoke pot?"

"Yeah."

"All of them?"

"Most of them."

"Lauren?"

"Yeah, I guess that's how I got started. The guys I know were already using pot, and then when I started seeing Lauren, and she was smoking, I decided to try it."

"Do her parents know?"

"I don't know—I guess not."

"It's wrong for you, Jody. I don't want you using drugs."

"Mom," O'Donnell interrupted, "you'd be asking Jody to be a hermit if you asked him to stop smoking pot altogether. He might as well go to his room and stay there. He would have nothing in common with his friends anymore."

"O'Donnell, you're the one who told me. You're the reason we're here talking about this, and now you say I shouldn't ask him to stop smoking pot." I was angry at O'Donnell for not supporting me.

"I just don't want him driving while he's using it."

"You don't use pot, do you?"

"No, but I'm different, and I have friends who don't."

"Well, if you have friends who don't, so can he."

"But all the people he's friends with and his girl friend do smoke pot." As O'Donnell continued to argue Jody's case, it occurred to me that O'Donnell probably felt guilty for telling on Jody. I didn't believe she felt that Jody should smoke pot any more than I did.

"Well, then, maybe he should get some new friends," I said out of frustration. I looked at Jody, and he was beginning to cry.

"Mom, you don't understand. It's not that bad. I think it's even good for me."

"I can't believe it, Jody. I'll never believe it. Do you and your friends do anything but get high when you go out?"

"No. There's nothing else to do. We drive somewhere, listen to music, and get high. What else is there to do?"

I was beginning to realize how little I knew about what my child had been doing when he said he was going out to a friend's house or to pick up Lauren or to a party. That didn't tell me what he was really doing.

I suggested alternatives. "There are movies and skiing and roller skating and parties without pot. There are plenty of things to do if you want to go to the trouble of finding them. I must admit there are no recreation centers around here to have dances in like those that there used to be when I was a teenager, but there are things to do."

"Even so, Mom, I'd still want to smoke pot. It makes me feel better. I have a better time. It relaxes me."

"Jody, your father used to have a drink or two before we went to a party to relax himself, to put himself 'in the mood' to party. I don't want to see you falling into the same pattern."

"The man is dead," O'Donnell shouted across the table as tears rolled down her face. "Will you please leave him alone?"

Now she was defending her father. Had she forgotten

how hard he was on her, how unpleasant he was to her at times?

"O'Donnell, I just want something better for Jody. I don't want to see him giving in to insecurities the way your father did. I want him to conquer them. I want a better life for Jody than your father had," I shouted back as tears now flowed from my eyes also.

"If you'd talk to us or spend more time with us, maybe we wouldn't be insecure. Sometimes you act more like a mother to other kids than you do to us," O'Donnell lashed out.

Where was this coming from, and why now, I thought.

"You're almost never home, and when you are, you hardly have time to talk to us"—she was continuing her attack. She was right, but I wasn't ready to admit it, even to myself.

"Let me tell you something," I said angrily, "if I didn't have to clean up after you all when I do get home, maybe I would have more time just to talk about *things*. If there weren't a pile of dishes waiting for me every night when I get home which I have to do before I start dinner, maybe we could get to know one another better and talk about what's bothering each of you and what's happening in your lives."

The charges and countercharges flowed as rapidly as the tears. Years of hurt burst out of my daughter like stuffing from the seams of an old chair after years of use and abuse. The purging of problems between my daughter and me continued for some time, and finally Jack, who had been quiet throughout, stepped in. He reached out with both hands, putting one on my arm and one on O'Donnell's.

"Take it easy, you two. That's enough. I think we've gotten off the track. I think we've lost sight of what we came to talk about. It's not bad for you to get these feelings out in the open, but we have another problem that we need to deal with right now. We need to come to some solution or compromise concerning Jody."

I got up to get a tissue to blow my nose and wipe the tears from my face, and there was Jody standing at the sink doing the breakfast dishes. I hadn't even noticed when he had gotten up from the table. The sight of him doing the dishes made me sob openly. I almost choked as I cried and gasped for breath at the same time. He *never* did the dishes. He was reacting to what I'd said to O'Donnell. He was doing something I normally did so I'd have time to talk to him, to be with him.

"Thank you, Jody," I said as I put my hands on his shoulders. "When you're finished, come back to the table so we can get something resolved with you."

I pulled some extra tissues from the box on the kitchen counter. As I handed them to O'Donnell I put my arms around her.

"I love you, O'Donnell, I really do. I'm sorry I haven't been a very good mother to you. I'll try to do better. I really will."

"I love you too, Mom."

We started to cry again. I held her in my arms, my face pressed tight against her head. We had opened a very deep wound and let out a lot of bitterness. I was feeling tremendous love and compassion for my daughter at that moment. I *had* spent much time being consumed with my career and my newfound freedom both before and after John's death. It was now apparent that O'Donnell and Jody and probably Marjorie had suffered greatly because of it.

I needed to be told the things she'd poured out. It's

painful to hear that you've let your kids down, but I wished she'd said it sooner. I just hoped it wasn't too late to make amends.

When Jody came back to the table I left O'Donnell's side and returned to my chair between Jody and Jack. I looked at Jack as I continued to dab at my eyes with the wet balled-up tissue.

"What are we going to do about Jody's pot smoking?" I asked.

"I don't know." Jack turned to Jody, "What do you suggest?"

"I want to go on doing it," Jody said matter-of-factly.

"Do you drive when you've been using it?" Jack asked Jody.

"Sometimes."

"That's very dangerous," Jack warned. "I know a lot of people who smoke pot think that their senses are sharper and their reflexes are better, but that's not true. Pot is a depressant. It slows you down; it takes you longer to react after you've smoked pot. People may think they're better drivers when they're using pot, but they aren't."

"You don't smoke pot when you're riding your motorcycle, do you?" I asked with alarm.

"No, Mom. I'm smarter than that. That's how Jimmy broke his leg, riding when he was high."

"Do you think you could use pot recreationally with your friends on weekends but not when you're driving?" Jack asked.

"I guess so," Jody said, less than convincingly.

"You said you use pot to study. What about that?" I asked.

"I'll try to cut down."

"How much are you using now?" I continued to question my son, still not believing the answers.

"A couple of joints a day."

"Every day?" I asked, astonished that this could be true.

"Yes," he answered honestly.

"And you will try to cut back, go some days without it?"

"Yes, I'll try," he said, starting to sound relieved as he realized I was not going to order him to stop using marijuana altogether. As I sat thinking about what was happening I began shaking my head. It was wrong. None of it sat well with me. But what was I going to do—ask my socially shy son to give up something all his friends were doing? Was I going to demand that he be different? Was he strong enough to be different? Would he obey me even if I did ask him to stop using pot? Would the peer pressure be stronger than my wishes? Would he hate me if I ordered him to stop? Would I have a better chance to stay close to him and maybe someday guide him away from drugs if I went along with pot in moderation? After all, the kids keep saying it's just like having a couple of beers. But a couple of beers *every day* would also be bad for a teenager.

"It's wrong, Jody. It's illegal, and it's not good for you. What I'm doing, going along with this, is wrong. I know it's not right, and yet I don't know what else to do. I'm just hoping you *will* cut back and someday not use it at all, and I hope and pray you don't really mess yourself up in the meantime. One more thing: I don't want to see you using pot. I don't approve, and I don't want to watch you doing it."

"Okay, Mom."

With those two words the discussion was over.

"I guess that's it, at least for today," I said, bringing the emotionally draining session to a close. Jody and O'Donnell got up and left the room. I looked at the clock. It was twelve o'clock. We had sat there talking and crying and pouring out our hearts and problems for three hours. My head ached and I barely had the strength to say another word. I just looked at Jack.

"How're you doing?" he asked as he took my hands in his.

"I don't know," I said. "Part of me hurts and part of me is numb."

"You really got it today."

"I'm afraid I deserved most of it. I just wish I'd had the strength to say no about the pot. But I couldn't somehow. Jody looked so desperate, so unhappy."

"I know what you mean," Jack said with sympathy. "My heart went out to him. He was really hurting today. I wanted him to know I cared for him. I wanted him to know I understood and sympathized with the pain he was experiencing."

"I think he knew. I think he felt it," I said.

"One thing we didn't ask him is where he gets the money to support his daily use of pot. That can get pretty expensive," Jack commented.

"Oh, I know where that comes from. I didn't need to ask," I replied. "I'm afraid I've always been too free with money. If he asks for gas money or something for his motorcycle racing, I give it to him, usually more than he needs. If he had to work for his money, he might be more careful how he spends it. That in itself might make him cut down on pot. This summer he's going to get a job," I said with conviction.

"In the meantime you can be more careful with the

money you give Jody and be certain what it's used for," Jack suggested.

"I will, but I don't want him to start selling things to support his habit or, worse yet, start dealing drugs to make money."

"I guess you're right."

"It's a mess," I said as I sat staring at the pictures on the kitchen wall, pictures of the kids when they were little. My eyes moved to a rough wooden plaque. Round tiles were glued on the wood in the shape of a tree. At the bottom of the plank in bold black letters was the name JODY. He had made the piece of artwork for me in kindergarten. Jack followed my gaze to the picture as I said, "It all seemed so easy then." Tears started to roll down my face again. "I wish I could start all over again"—I paused and looked at Jack—"with you."

"So do I," he said. He turned to look at the clock on the wall at the other end of the kitchen.

"Speaking of kids, I've got to pick up Christopher at his mother's."

"Do you want to bring him back here for dinner?" I asked.

"Sure," said Jack. "But are you up to fixing dinner tonight?"

"I'll be all right. I'm going to take some aspirin and lie down for a little while."

Jack left, and I walked upstairs to take a nap. Before I went to my bedroom I stepped into O'Donnell's room.

"Are you all right?" I asked.

"Yes, Mom. I'm all right."

"I hope so. I really do love you, you know."

"I know. I love you too, Mom."

I walked out of O'Donnell's room and went to the third

floor to see Jody. Rock music was coming from the tape deck, not as loud as usual because Jody had been on the phone. He was hanging it up as I walked up the stairs.

"Making plans for tonight?" I asked.

"Yeah. I'm going to a party with Lauren."

"Where's the party going to be?"

"Some friend of hers from school—nobody you'd know."

"No, I guess not." I paused to choose my words carefully. "Jody, I'm glad we had the discussion today. I'm not happy about the pot, but I'm glad I know about it. I want you to know I love you, no matter what." I walked closer to him and put my arms around him. "And I'm going to start hugging you more. I don't care if you are almost seventeen and bigger than I am."

He smiled and his arms tightened around me. We stood there holding each other for a few minutes, enjoying the comfort of being close. We had done far too little of this.

I walked back downstairs and into my room. My head was throbbing now as I lay down on the bed. He's going to a party tonight, I thought. I guess he'll get high. Oh, God, I think I've made a terrible mistake. Tears rolled out onto the pillow as I closed my eyes and tried to go to sleep.

Jody needed professional help right then. I needed help. Jody's life was out of control, and I didn't know how to guide him or how to handle the problem myself. I thought my love for my son was strong enough to see him through. Love does not conquer all.

The family discussion that aired the problem of pot and exposed other suppressed feelings was good. It had a cleansing effect, even therapeutic, on all of us. But it would probably have accomplished a lot more if it had been done in the presence of a psychologist, psychiatrist, counselor, or minister—someone outside the family who is trained to handle such a situation, a person who could guide constructively and offer advice and direction when those emotionally involved are floundering.

Even if the first discussion had not been conducted with a professional, I should have sought help immediately after that. It should have been clear to me that we were in real trouble. Not only was there Jody's car accident, which I believe was caused because he had been smoking marijuana, but the incident at St. Paul's happened right around the time when he says he started using pot. I think he was expelled from school because of something he did while under the influence of dope. And it finally dawned on me why he spent so much time away from us at the beach. He and his friends were getting high and he didn't want me to know it. Jody was using marijuana to escape the pain in his life—the pain from his father's death and the pain and insecurity that came from simply being a teenager.

The pot and smoking it with his friends also eased the loneliness in his life, helped him through the many hours of being by himself because I was away from home so much of the time pursuing a career and a relationship with Jack. I had tried to deal with Jody's loneliness several times. But I didn't try hard enough, and for that I will always be sorry. I didn't go out during the week after I got home from work. However, since I was required to work until seven-thirty each evening, I didn't get home until about eight-fifteen. It wasn't so bad when Jody was staying at his cousin's. But when he started driving his own car to school, he'd come home to an empty house about four. He'd do homework and usually go out again to a friend's house until he knew it was time for me to be home to fix dinner.

189

One night I got home first, and when he came in I said, "Do you have to go to Eddie's house every day?"

"Well, I'm not staying here alone," he had said sharply.

I knew then what I had felt all along, that I should have taken a stand with the station management on the issue of my hours a long time before.

Years earlier I had asked if I could work a regular eight-hour day—nine to five, or better yet, eight to four. I knew I could do the same reports; I just wouldn't be "live" at seven.

The general manager at that time said, "If you want to work nine to five, get a job as a secretary. This is TV news. It happens at six and seven."

If my bosses had insisted that they must have me live at that hour or not at all, I should have left and found another job. I don't think if I had pushed, really pushed, for more suitable hours they would have let me go. But I didn't do that. You can be sure I would today if I had it to do over. Obviously for Jody it was easier not to cope with the problems and the pain and the loneliness but instead to do something a lot of other kids were also doing—some for similar reasons and some who were just going along with the crowd.

Jack says he didn't suggest that Jody should be forbidden to use pot because he wanted my son to like him. But he has since said that if Jody had been his son, he would have handled the situation entirely differently. He says he would have laid down the law. He would not have allowed him to use it for any reason. At the time he was afraid Jody would resent him if he came on too strong. He didn't want Jody to think he didn't understand that there were kids and adults using marijuana for recreation and that they seemed to be okay. He wanted to be a good guy in

Jody's eyes. He wanted to be his friend. I too wanted Jody to go on loving me. I didn't want to do something that would alienate him.

There are many of us caring, loving, well-meaning parents who are killing our kids with kindness. Being a buddy doesn't work when children are fooling around with drugs and alcohol. Too many teenagers aren't letting themselves grow up. They aren't letting themselves feel the pain and joy of passing through puberty so that they come out on the other side as well-adjusted, mature adults.

The natural highs and lows of life need to be dealt with in order for kids to grow into healthy human beings. Pills, alcohol, and pot are all being used to fake the growing process. If a boy is nervous about calling a girl for a date, he can take something and he'll be cool. If that girl wants to be smooth and sophisticated on the date and maybe even say yes to sex she's really not ready to try, she uses something to tear down those inhibitions. Chemicals are controlling the minds and bodies of many of our kids, and after years of use, when they are physically old enough to be called adults and take responsibility for their lives, they are emotionally and perhaps physically incapable of doing so!

Parents don't do their kids any favors by allowing them to use drugs and alcohol. The kids may feel "with it" at fifteen, but they may feel very much "without it" at twenty-one—without the inner resources to live a productive life or even sometimes to live at all. Actress Carol Burnett put it simply when, talking about her daughter's use of drugs and the struggle to help her child overcome her habit, she said, "You have to love your kids enough to let them hate you for a little while." And that means saying no and getting help if necessary to make it stick.

*I have also come to believe that kids want their parents
to say no. It shows children that someone cares about them.
It says to the children that their mothers and fathers love
them enough to want to protect them. Always letting children do what they say they want to do, especially letting
them make decisions in regard to such major issues as drug
use, having sex, and staying out very late, sends the child
the message that the parent doesn't really care what they do.*

*Setting rules and saying no can also relieve children of
the burden of making adult decisions that they may not be
prepared to make on their own. If they can say, "My parents won't let me do that," or "I promised my parents I
wouldn't do that," it frees them from peer pressure. If a
teenage girl just starting to date can say, "I have to be
home by midnight or I can't go out next weekend," she
has an excuse that can help her avoid any number of
sticky situations. And if she knows her parents are waiting
up for her, concerned about her safety, she'll not only get
home on time, she'll know her parents love her enough to
give up a little sleep. She might complain about being
treated like a baby, but the feeling of security, of caring,
has been transmitted and received—that is, if the teen is
always given love, respect, and rules, but not subjected to
mistrust, accusations, and unreasonable demands. And, of
course, a good example is worth a thousand words, hundreds of rules, and dozens of reprimands. I feel I failed in
this area as well as in many others.*

*The wineglass sitting on my bedside table night after
night said more to my son about adult behavior and what
I thought was acceptable than any words I spoke to the
contrary. You simply cannot say to a teenager today, "Do
as I say, not as I do," and expect to have a nondrinking,
drug-free, morally straight, rational, respectable kid if you*

yourself are living another kind of existence. If booze is a daily part of your life, if divorce has thrown you back into the dating game, with late hours and rotating bed partners, your teenager could be in trouble. You may be teaching your teen the exact opposite of what you want him or her to be.

Sooner or later most kids end up imitating their parents. We may not like it, but I believe our life-styles are our legacies to our children—much more so than the lip service we give to precepts we expect them to live by.

CHAPTER 9

SHE LOVES ME, SHE LOVES ME NOT

APRIL 1977

*J*ODY had never cared much about clothes. He had to wear a coat and tie when he was at St. Paul's, but I usually picked them out. He wasn't choosy, and he didn't care if he wore the same coat and tie every day. But now jeans were his uniform, just as they were for every other kid his age. I usually bought them without his being along. But suddenly we were on a shopping spree, and every item of clothing called for a major decision.

Jody was in love, deeply and overwhelmingly in love. His feelings for Lauren affected everything he did. He was worried about *her* likes and dislikes. Her wants and desires were becoming his own, and Jody's inclinations were no longer the primary consideration in the choices he made concerning what he did and the way he lived.

"I don't know, Mom. I haven't seen anybody wearing these kind of pants or wearing vests."

"You will, believe me, you will. You'll be seeing more

people in these styles in the next couple of months. They're showing these things in all the fashion magazines."

"I like them," Jody was saying, as if to placate me, "but I'm not sure I should wear them."

"Well, don't," I said. "I don't want to buy something you're not going to wear." After what seemed like hours of hemming and hawing and looking at the outfit from every imaginable angle in the full-length mirror, Jody decided he would take it. He bought that outfit along with several pairs of Levi's and cotton shirts, which I knew he would wear. We also bought two silk shirts similar to those he had seen on other young men at the motorcycle awards banquet. I knew Jody would never wear them, but I bought them anyway in hopes he might crawl out of his conservative shell. I had the feeling that nothing would be worn until it was approved by Lauren.

"Maybe we should have brought Lauren with us on this shopping spree?" I said with a smile and a raised eyebrow as we drove home. "Then it wouldn't have taken so long and we could be sure you'd wear what she picked out."

Jody just looked at me and turned up the stereo in his car.

We were now a four-car family. O'Donnell had gotten permission to take the Honda back to college with her, and I had bought Jody a used Mustang, a snappy red-and-black hatchback with fluted back-window shades and the orange-and-black decal of the Mustang on the front fenders—a car, I told Jody, that was sure to catch the cops' eyes, so he'd better drive within the speed limit. I went against every instinct and John's wishes when I bought the car. I knew John didn't want his son to have his own car until he worked for the money to buy it. John felt it was more important for a boy to do this than a girl. I don't know if I agree with that, but I do agree that it's much wiser if a teenager, male or female, works and saves to buy his or her first car. But once again I rationalized: Jody needed the car because of my work schedule. The truth is that O'Donnell didn't have to take the Honda to college, and even if she did, Jody and I could have shared my car. He could have taken me to the station before going to school and picked me up after work; or sometimes Jack could have taken me home. It would have been a little inconvenient, but it may have been better for us all.

I turned the radio down.

"Jody, I can't stand *that* music *that* loud."

He laughed and turned it up again. It was a game we usually played when I was riding in his car. He loved to tease me by turning the rock music up so loud you literally could not think and conversation was impossible. I turned it down.

"Jody, I mean it. I've got a headache, and that's making it worse." He didn't turn it up again. "Don't forget, you've got to take me to the store before we go home. I need a few things for dinner."

"Maah-um. I've got to call Lauren. I told her I'd call about three, and it's almost that now."

"Lauren will have to wait, or you can call her from the phone in the A&P. I have to get something for dinner."

Jody decided to wait until he got home to call Lauren. I imagine he was uncomfortable using the pay phone in a supermarket, where people were around while he talked to his girl friend. At the A&P he waited impatiently in the car while I hurriedly grabbed what I needed to fix dinner. I didn't take time to shop for other things. I'd do that another day when Jody wasn't with me. I'd wanted to get food for Jody to eat while I was in Annapolis at the end of the following week, but I could do that the coming Monday or Tuesday.

Driving home, I once again asked Jody if he wouldn't reconsider and go to Annapolis with me. For the past couple of years I had gone down to the state capital for the close of the ninety-day session of the legislature. Jack was there covering the last-minute flurry of activity, and I found it fun to take a few days' vacation and become a spectator for a change rather than a reporter. Annapolis is a charming old waterfront town with a cosmopolitan air about it, lots of shops, excellent restaurants, and small pubs with good music. It was very pleasant to spend a few days there, and it would be great to have Jody along.

"How about it, Jody? We'd have a good time. Remember when I took you to Annapolis, when your father and I were separated? Remember, we went on the harbor boat tour out around the Naval Academy? I learned things on that tour I'd never known before. It was fun, wasn't it?"

"Yeah."

"We could do that again, and we could even rent a sailboat. How long's it been since we've been sailing? Ages. Since we were in Cape May, when you were just learning to sail, when you tried to drown me by capsizing the boat."

We smiled. That thought brought back happy memories for both of us. Just the two of us on a little sunfish, Jody showing me what he had learned in sailing class. First we had a hard time getting the boat to leave the shore. The wind kept blowing us back to land. Jody was so frustrated. The harder he tried to do what he'd been taught, the quicker we would be blown back to shore. Finally I pushed the boat out into the bay, saying, "I make a better motor than you do a sailor."

Then he delighted in showing me how easily a sunfish can be turned over and how easily it can be righted. Once would have been enough, but not for Jody. It was too much fun to hear me scream and watch me splash in the water. It was a pleasant memory for us now—the two of us laughing and hanging onto the boat, getting it upright, only to have it tip over again.

"Come on, Jody, we'd have a good time. It works out perfectly. You're having spring break the same time."

"Naw, Mom, not this year. It's my vacation too, and I want to spend it here with Lauren."

"Well, then, I've got a great idea. Why don't you and Lauren drive down to Annapolis on Thursday or Friday? We'll do something like a boat tour or watch the senators and delegates perform, and then Jack and I will take you to dinner."

"No, I don't think so. I think I just want to stay here, and I don't think Lauren would want to go."

"Okay, but if you change your mind, you know I'd love to have you join us."

"I know, Mom."

When we got home Jody rushed upstairs to make his call to Lauren from the phone on the third floor. About fifteen minutes later he came down, and as he was walking through the kitchen to go out the back door to the motorcycle shed, he said, "Now she doesn't want to go out tonight." He seemed crestfallen.

"What do you mean?" I asked.

"She says she's made other plans. She says when I didn't call at three, she thought I wasn't interested or that I was doing something else tonight."

"That's ridiculous," I said. "She knew you wanted to go

out with her. You were just calling to find out what she wanted to do. Right?"

"That's right. But that's how she is."

Jody walked out the back door, and I watched through the window as he headed for the motorcycle shed to get his bike ready for tomorrow's race.

That bitch, I thought. She called him and chased him until she had him wrapped around her little finger, and now she's playing with his emotions like a Yo-Yo at the end of a string. I wonder if she has any idea how much he cares about her. At Jody's seventeenth birthday celebration in March she'd been gushing over him like a new bride and even talking about being a good wife for him someday. Now she'd made other plans because he hadn't called promptly at three when he was supposed to. Well, she's only fifteen, I thought. She doesn't know what she's doing or what she wants. She's playing a grown-up game without really knowing the rules or what the stakes are. I should know because I was blindly playing the same game with Jody's father when *I* was fifteen.

Romance is fun, love is powerful, but commitment in the changing life of a teenager is complicated at best. Most fifteen-year-olds don't know what they want to do with their lives, so how can they possibly know with whom they want to share that unforeseeable life? Our interests and personalities change as we grow and so do the attractions of those who appeal to us as possible mates. But the feelings can be strong at fifteen or sixteen or seventeen, although we don't understand them and perhaps aren't comfortable with them yet. They can confuse us and they can cause us to be very cruel. They can even lead some, like me, into a premature marriage.

When both people involved feel equally in love, there is nothing on earth more wonderful. But if the love isn't returned or one feels more strongly than the other, nothing in the world can cause more pain. We learn to deal with that and accept it as we mature. We learn through experience that there can be another love, another person with whom we can share a close relationship; one even stronger and more special than the one before. But when we are teenagers and we feel love for the first time, it's easy to think that our first love will be our last. 'There's only one bit of advice I offer young people to lessen the pain and heighten the joy of romance. Don't use the power of love to feed your own ego. If you cannot return someone's love or commitment, get out of that person's life as quickly and as gently as possible. Don't toy with emotions; it can be very dangerous.

The phone was ringing. I turned away from the window and my thoughts.

"Hello."

"Hello. Is Jody there?" It was Lauren.

"Yes, Lauren, but he's out in the motorcycle shed getting his bike ready for tomorrow's race."

"Oh, where's the race tomorrow? I'd love to go."

"It's at Big Berm."

"Oh, good. That's not too far away."

"Lauren, would you like me to have Jody call you when he comes in?"

"Oh, yes, Mrs. White, if you would, please."

I hung up the phone as Jody was walking in the back door.

"Did I hear the phone ring?" he asked.

"Yes, and guess who it was."

"Lauren."

"Right. She wants you to call her, and she said she wants to go to the race tomorrow."

"Okay," he said, his spirits obviously brightened. He walked out of the kitchen and ran up the stairs to his room to call her back. When he came down again he was all smiles.

"Can we have dinner early? Lauren wants me to take her shopping and then to a party."

"What changed her mind?"

"I don't know. That's just the way she is."

She probably couldn't get anyone else to take her, I thought, but didn't say it. When Jody was happy I wasn't about to burst his balloon.

"Sure, you can have dinner early. What time?"

"About five-thirty."

"Okay, but don't forget you've got a race tomorrow, so don't be too late coming in tonight."

"I don't need a lot of sleep. I'm better if I haven't had too much sleep."

"Don't give me that, and don't be out all night."

"I won't."

I also wanted to say and didn't, "Stay straight—you need a clear head to race."

I had said nothing to Jody about the pot smoking since our big discussion in January. I was afraid to, once again afraid of what he might say and how I would handle it if I heard something I didn't like. He hadn't at any time come home stoned and out of control. His grades hadn't dropped. I was hoping he had eased off marijuana and wasn't abusing it.

I was sidestepping my job as a parent—that's what I was really doing. I was hoping everything was going along all right, but I didn't know because I didn't ask. After the family discussion about pot I had vowed we would have more such sessions. But I let the idea slide. I didn't initiate any more talks. The one in January had been so emotionally draining. Each time I thought about starting another, I decided I didn't have the strength for it "right then"; maybe next week. There's always next week, I'd tell myself. As soon as I get back from Annapolis, I told myself, I'm going to find out if he's still smoking pot and how much. I think we'll also get into his relationship with Lauren, and sex too. He's seventeen years old and I've never really had a talk with him about sex. He's had no father to talk to for the past two and a half years, two and a half important years when he probably had a lot of questions about sex. I suppose he got the answers from his friends. I shouldn't let these things slide, I thought, scolding myself. Kids don't just grow up knowing instinctively what's going on with their bodies and how to deal with it. I'll get Jack in on that discussion. He's good at explaining things, and I think some explaining and talking definitely needs to be done.

The night of Jody's birthday dinner, when I went up to my son's room to tell him dinner was ready, I was rather shocked at what I found. He and Lauren were rolling around on his bed. Jody's hands were all over her, and Lauren was squirming and giggling. They were fully dressed, but their faces flushed when I walked in on them. Jody said they were wrestling. Lauren just giggled some more. It hit me then that Jody and Lauren were probably already having sex together. For some reason it had never crossed my mind until that moment. But did I say anything? Did I use the incident as an opportunity to find out more about what was going on in my son's life? Did

I even make sure if he was having sex with Lauren or with anyone else, that he was taking precautions so he didn't get anyone pregnant? No. I avoided talking about the incident and sex in general because I wasn't sure what to say.

I was thinking about that as I sat on a little secluded beach on the banks of the Severn River in Annapolis. I had left the noise and legislative posturing at the State House and sought out the solitude of this picturesque spot. It was warm for April. The sun was a comfort to my winter-weary body, even if it couldn't melt away the worries on my mind. Sailboats danced on the river, some cutting through the water fairly close to shore. Others filled the horizon like a chorus line. The sun glittered and bounced off the river, almost seeming to keep in time with the motion of the boats. As I watched them I wished once again that Jody had come with me. Maybe it would have been a good time for a long talk, just the two of us. It would also have given him a couple of days away from Lauren for some long-distance thoughts about their relationship. But I knew all he wanted was to be with her, and I imagine the thought of having her and the house to himself without me around to walk in on them was more exciting than coming to Annapolis with his mother.

I also knew that what he wanted was not necessarily good for him nor would it make him happy. However, *my* knowing it did Jody absolutely no good. I got up and walked slowly back down the little stretch of sand to where I had parked my car. I would do a little shopping before meeting Jack at the condo, which was serving as the Channel 2 Annapolis Bureau. We would go out and have a pleasant dinner, and the next day I would go home and have that long overdue talk with Jody.

Getting that course of action squared away in my mind somehow allowed me to relax and enjoy the evening. We had dinner at a wonderful small French restaurant and held hands across a table bathed in candlelight and decorated with roses. I didn't mention my thoughts and concerns about Jody. I didn't dare. I was afraid it might rekindle some unpleasant thoughts of a few weeks ago. Jack hadn't come to Jody's birthday dinner, and it had upset me very much. He'd called at the last minute and said Christopher wasn't feeling well and he was going to see him instead. As always, I had made something special of Jody's birthday. I'd decided that for his seventeenth birthday a grown-up dinner with steak and champagne and candlelight was in order. Lauren was going to be there— her first dinner with us—and some of Jody's other friends were invited. I very much wanted Jack there, and when he called and said he couldn't come, he spoiled the night for me. Later I accused him of always putting his son first and never considering my son. He said that if the evening was so important to me, I should have told him, that I couldn't expect him to be a mind reader about what was important to me or my children, which I agreed was true. But I was still very upset. It had been distinctly unpleasant, and I didn't want to chance bringing those feelings to the surface again by talking about Jody.

It was one of those times when I felt torn between my concerns and love for Jody and my deepening love for Jack. I opted to push my thoughts of my son aside to indulge in a problem-free night of love. It was a wonderful evening and sent my spirits soaring.

I was still smiling the next day as I drove home. As I pulled into the driveway I drove my car to the side of the house so I could take my suitcase and the gifts I'd bought the kids in the back door.

Jody's car was parked out front. Great, I thought, he's home. I'm looking forward to seeing him. I had a good time, but I sure missed my son. I was leaning in the back door of the car getting the gifts off the back seat when I heard the engine of Jody's car start up. I dropped the things in my hands and ran to the top of the hill to cut Jody off as he started to move out of the driveway. I was waving my hands as I ran so he would see me. The car was still moving as I grabbed the handle on the passenger's side and yanked open the door. The car stopped. I got in, saying, "Hey, where are you going? I just got home and I want to see you."

Jody turned to face me.

"My God," I said, "you look awful. What's wrong?"

Jody's eyes were red and swollen. He had been crying. There were dark circles under his eyes, as if he hadn't slept in days, and he was gaunt, as if he hadn't eaten. He began to cry again as he spoke.

"Sometimes she loves me, and sometimes she doesn't, and when she doesn't she won't tell me why. I've got to talk to her. Please let me go. I've got to talk to her. I've got to make her explain what she's feeling. I've got to make her understand how much I love her. She won't talk to me on the phone. I've got to get over to her house before she goes out. I've got to make her understand."

My son's pain touched me so deeply I could barely speak. I choked out my advice. "Jody, don't go over there like this. It will just drive Lauren further away. It won't do any good to talk to her when you're in this condition. To see you crying like this and to hear you begging will just be more of a turnoff for someone like Lauren. She's been playing with you for some time. I'm afraid she's the kind who wants what she can't have, then when she gets it, she steps all over it. Don't go over there and show her that she's beaten you down like this. Let's go back inside and talk about it. Get yourself together, then go to see her. Please."

Jody put his car in reverse and backed into the parking space. He got out and walked into the house. God, I thought, how am I going to help him? I would give my life if he didn't have to feel such pain. I would do anything or buy him anything to make life more pleasant for him. But money can't buy relief from this hurt. I can't kiss this hurt and make it go away. I had been in Annapolis having a good time while he was up here suffering. I sobbed as I rested my forehead on the dashboard of my son's car. I wished I had forced him to go with me. But how do you force a seventeen-year-old to do anything? What I should have done was stay home. I didn't need to go, with Jody home alone depending only on Lauren for company. I got out of his car, went over to mine, took the things out of it, and walked into the house to try to say something that would ease Jody's pain. Maybe I could find the right words to help him deal with this. After all, he had done what I'd asked and hadn't gone to Lauren's.

I went up the stairs to the third floor carrying the gift I'd bought for Jody in Annapolis. It was a tin candle holder shaped like a coffee can; a design had been cut around the sides so that the light from the candle inside would shine through. Jody was into candles and other dim lights, such as red and blue bulbs. I don't know if it was because he was a pot smoker and that went along with incense burning or if it was just a fad of all teens during this period. If he liked candles because they were romantic, this was the wrong time to give him such a gift, but I had bought it for him, and I thought it might cheer him up. I also wanted him to know I had at least been thinking about him.

Jody was lying on his bed staring at the ceiling. He didn't even have his stereo on. I sat down beside him and handed him the gift. It was wrapped in tissue paper with a ribbon around it.

"I thought you might like this. I found it in a neat little craft shop down in Annapolis."

Jody pushed himself into a half-sitting position, leaning his head and back against the wall. I watched as he carefully untied the ribbon and unwrapped the paper. Jody did everything neatly. He was one of those rare boys who kept everything in his dresser drawers in perfect order: shirts, underwear, socks, all folded carefully and stacked in little piles. Items on top of the dresser and on his shelves were also arranged just where he wanted them. Everything had a place and everything was always kept in its place. John was like that, and so is Marjorie—the kind of people who very much need order in their lives. There was no mental or emotional order in Jody's life right now, and I desperately wanted to help him regain it.

Jody was looking at the candle holder.

"I thought it might put a little light into your life," I joked.

He smiled.

"Besides," I went on, "you can burn a candle in there without taking a chance on burning the house down. The flame is protected, and when the candle melts down inside the tin container, the fire goes out."

"It's neat, Mom, thank you."

"I'm glad you like it. I wish I had something to really make you happy right now."

He slumped down on his bed and lay flat on his back.

"Jody, I know this may not mean anything to you right now and it may sound trite, but Lauren is not the only girl in the world. There are lots of girls who would give everything to go out with Jody White. You've got a lot going for you, and you've got a lot to offer a girl. You're handsome, intelligent, athletic, fun to be with, and if all that isn't enough, you race motorcycles and you have your own car. Dozens of girls would be proud to be Jody White's girl friend."

"But I don't want dozens of girls. I want Lauren." Tears returned to his eyes.

"Oh, Jody, I wish I could take this pain from you." I put my hand on his face, wiped away the tears, and brushed his hair off his forehead. "I love you so much it hurts me just knowing how much you're suffering. You think that there'll never be another person in your life like Lauren, but there will be—even better. Look at me. If anybody had told me when I was your age that the deepest most wonderful love in my life would occur after I was thirty-five, I'd have said that person was crazy, that it couldn't happen. But it has happened. I know it doesn't help ease the pain you're feeling, but you're not alone. Lots of teenagers go through what you're going through right now. Unfortunately it's part of growing up. We can't make people love us or be nice to us. When someone rejects us, we have to try to forget about it and go on— eventually to someone else.

It was probably stupid and certainly insensitive to mention my love for Jack at that moment. Jody was probably feeling very unlovable as it was. I must have accentuated

those thoughts. I had gone to Annapolis and left him
alone. Lauren had decided she didn't want to see him any-
more. Who did want to be with him? It must have seemed
to him that no one did. By mentioning my love for Jack
I must have fueled his feelings that Jack was more impor-
tant to me than he was, just as Jack had been more im-
portant to me than his father was.

I should have chosen my words more carefully, knowing
that I was walking on emotional eggshells. But I wanted
Jody to know that there could and most likely would be
another girl friend in his life.

"I don't want someone else, Mom. I can talk to her. She
makes me feel good," he was saying.

"And right now she's making you feel very bad. Jody,
if you go to her and cry and beg, she'll have no respect for
you. She'll just reject you again. I hate to suggest you play
games, but that's what you have to do with some people.
If you're ever to get her back, you're going to have to pre-
tend you don't care about her. You'll have to appear to be
indifferent. Remember how she was when you really didn't
care. She called every five minutes. She wouldn't leave you
alone.

"But I'll tell you, I think you'd be better off just to forget Miss Lauren. She's going to do nothing but hurt you.
It'll take a while for the pain to stop, but believe me, it
will stop. Someday you'll stop thinking about her, stop
wanting to be with her. Oh, you'll remember her. We always remember our first real love, but it will no longer
hurt to picture her in your mind. Please do me one favor,
no matter what you decide. Don't call her or go to see her
today or tomorrow. A week would be better. You need
some time away from her to get yourself together. She
needs some time without you pursuing her to think about

what you mean to her and if she wants to go on seeing you or not. Can you do that for me?"

"I guess so."

"Good. Now I'm going down to fix you something to eat. You look as if you haven't eaten since I left."

Jody didn't say whether he had or hadn't. He just stared at the ceiling, at the candle holder in his hands. I reached down and took it from him.

"I'll put a candle in this and bring it back. Maybe a red or blue one. Which do you think?"

"I don't care—red, I guess."

"Red it will be. Do you want me to bring your food up here or will you come down for it?"

"I'm really not hungry, Mom."

"Well, I don't care. You're going to eat something whether you're hungry or not. I'll bring it up."

I walked downstairs staring at the candle holder as I went and thinking, Why Jody? Why does someone as sensitive as he is who has already had enough pain in his life have to fall in love with someone who doesn't return his love? There are so many others, and he'll meet them, I thought. I just have to get him over this one, and that's not going to be easy. But we'll make it. One Egg McWhite and things will look a whole lot brighter.

One Egg McWhite was not the cure-all and neither was my continuous babbling. I kept running to Jody's room explaining things—for instance, how I felt when I was fourteen and a boy I liked rejected me. Once again I did all the talking. Never did I just sit with my son and say, "How are you feeling? What are your thoughts? Do you want to talk?" and wait for him to get it out. He was depressed and he needed desperately to talk to someone about his feelings so that he could understand them. He would come home from school and just lie on his bed and brood. I'd come home, run upstairs, and try to cheer him up. I think he eventually built a wall around himself and his depression to hide it from me. As the days passed I felt I was seeing an improvement in Jody's moods. He seemed brighter, less sad. But I think his deep-seated unhappiness was being camouflaged to please me, to ease my worry and shut me up so that I would stop talking about it.

By the end of April Jody did seem less depressed. He had apparently stopped seeing Lauren and was going over to Eddie's again, even going out with the guys to parties, where he had a chance to meet other girls. We were making plans for the new moto-cross racing season. I had bought him a new motorcycle, keeping my promise to get him a new bike each year with my tax refund. And that seemed to put a spark back in his life.

I was encouraged. I felt things really were improving in Jody's world. I sure hoped they were. I would just keep my fingers crossed that something wonderful would happen to bring real happiness to my son.

CHAPTER 10

THE RACE TO THE END

THE END OF APRIL,
THE FIRST OF MAY 1977

"*DO YOU* want to take your car or mine
to the races tomorrow?" I asked
Jody as we sat at breakfast the last Saturday in April. It
was a perfectly beautiful day, the kind of day that inspires
poetry and songs. I had already been outside working in
the flower beds, pulling weeds and picking daffodils. I had
put a big bouquet in the center of the kitchen table.

"Look at these gorgeous daffodils," I said to Jody, not
even letting him answer my question. "Look how many
different varieties I have."

"They're great, Mom."

"I'm glad you think so. I can always count on you to
appreciate the finer things in life," I teased.

"I'll take my car with the trailer and motorcycle early,
and you can come over later, right before the races start,"
Jody told me.

"That's okay, but I don't mind getting up early. I kind
of enjoy it."

"Well . . . Lauren wants to go to the races with me tomorrow, and I told her I'd pick her up about seven-thirty."

"Lauren?" I said with surprise.

"Yeah. I saw her at a party last night and she said she'd like to see me race again."

"Oh? Do you think that's a good idea?"

"I really like Lauren, Mom, and I want to be with her if she wants to be with me."

"Okay," I said hesitantly and with grave reservations. "I'll meet you at the track."

The next morning I heard Jody's alarm go off at six-thirty. I listened as he came down the steps trying to be quiet. It was only four hours ago that he had gone up those steps, also trying to be quiet. He had been out late, much too late for the night before a race.

I was worried about Jody again. When I allowed myself to look beneath the "I'm okay" facade, which he was displaying at that time, I saw emotional and physical deterioration. There had been a slow but steady decline in his appearance. His hair was getting longer. A sloppy teenager or one with an emotional problem who was heavily into drugs? His eyes looked glazed much of the time, and he was becoming very forgetful. I was scared, but I didn't know what to do, so I tried to remain calm and hoped and prayed it was just a phase that would pass. Why I didn't seek professional help at that point I will never, never be able to understand. I simply don't know where my rational adult mind was.

I called to Jody as he passed my bedroom door on the way to the bathroom.

"Would you like me to fix your breakfast?"

"No, we'll stop at McDonald's after I pick up Lauren."

"Jody, you were out much too late last night. There's no way you're going to be able to race your best today."

"I'll handle it. I'll be all right."

"Even if you do, it's not good for you to try to expend all that energy without a good night's rest. It's dangerous."

"I'll be all right, Mom."

I let the subject drop.

I wanted him to continue to have his motorcycle racing. I felt if he had that, he had something to hold onto. And perhaps I reasoned that if he could race, things might not be as bad as I thought.

"Okay, I'll see you over there."

It was about ten-thirty when I got to Big Berm Raceway. The practice sessions had already been held and the first moto for the 125 C class was on the starting line. I had plenty of time before Jody's first race. There were two twenty-minute races before the 125 expert class. He wouldn't even have his boots on yet. I made my way from the car to the pit area, past hundreds of motorcycles, trailers, campers, and vans, some with colorful canopies extending out from the sides. I knew many of the riders and spoke to them as I passed.

"Hi, have you seen where Jody is parked?"

"He's about six places down, back toward that big tree."

I looked through the maze of multicolored motorcycles and kids dressed in racing garb and spied Jody's red Mustang, with his bright yellow Suzuki leaning up against the trailer behind the car.

As I got closer I saw that Eddie and his family were parked on one side of Jody's car. Tommy and his girl friend were on the other side. Eddie and Tommy, like most of the other riders, were out working on their bikes, tuning them up, tightening the chains, making other last-minute adjustments. Jody, however, was sitting in his car with Lauren listening to rock music on his car stereo. He opened his door as I approached.

"Hello," I said to Jody. I leaned down and looked over at Lauren. "Hi, Lauren. It's good to see you again."

"It's good to see you again too."

"You all ready?" I asked Jody.

"Yeah. I missed practice though."

"How come?"

"Well, Lauren wasn't quite ready when I got to her house. Then we stopped for breakfast, and then we were hurrying to get here and a cop stopped me."

"Oh, no, Jody. Did he give you a ticket?"

"Yeah. I was doing sixty in a forty-mile zone."

"Pulling a motorcycle trailer! That's not too bright, Jody."

"I was late. I was afraid I would miss sign-up."

"That's no excuse. Well, there goes your perfect record."

"And forty bucks," Jody added. "You gonna pay it for me?"

"We'll see. We'll talk about that later. You need me to help you with anything to get ready for your first moto?"

"Naw, I'm all ready. I did everything yesterday, plus it's a new bike. What's to be done?"

"All right, then I'm going over on the hill where I can get some good pictures. Good luck and *be careful!*"

I was really afraid that Jody might get hurt on this day—and not only because of his lack of sleep. He hadn't raced in several months, not since he had broken his arm in a motorcycle accident in our driveway right after Christmas. He and his friend Dean ran into each other, a head-on collision. Both were going fast, and I had a feeling they were playing chicken, a game in which they would drive toward each other and at the last minute swerve their bikes to avoid a collision. They denied that they were doing that. They told me that Jody was going out the road just as Dean was riding in and that they both came around the blind turn at the top of the hill at precisely the same moment. They said it was one of those freak accidents that was impossible to avoid, that with the loud sound of the motorcycle engines, there was no way to know where the other rider was. But both boys were too experienced in riding and racing and too aware of motorcyclists' safety rules for me to quite believe that story. They knew that when riding into a blind turn one always stays to the right. I think they got caught playing a dangerous game of macho versus machine.

Jody had broken his arm and sprained his leg. He had ended up with a cast on his arm and walking on crutches, which wasn't exactly easy to manage, because he had to maneuver the crutches without using his broken arm.

To get in shape for this race Jody had been riding his motorcycle around the farm and practicing on his moto-cross course at home. He had also been using a hand grip to exercise and strengthen his injured arm, but I knew this first race was not going to be easy. It called for thirty minutes of hard riding, with the arms taking much of the brutal impact of going over jumps and riding a rough moto-cross course. They act almost like shock absorbers for the rest of the body; in addition, the right hand, which is the one Jody broke, is constantly in motion, controlling the throttle.

Jody had his arm taped with heavy-duty repair tape. He also had his leg taped. My main concern, however, was not whether his arm and leg would hold up but rather, would he? He just wasn't in as good shape as he once had been. Not that his body had gotten soft, but his ability to endure long periods of strenuous physical exertion had diminished considerably. I had noticed that the weekend before this race when I had asked him to help me cut down some trees. Holding the chain saw and bending over to cut the logs tired him much too quickly. At one point he'd even appeared to get dizzy and had had to sit down and rest. He had gotten in late the night before, and God only knows what his body was sweating out as he cut the trees. My stamina seemed better than his—a thirty-seven-year-old woman seemingly with more endurance than a seventeen-year-old boy. That just wasn't right. Something was drastically wrong with my son.

But what did I do? I stopped work and took him inside and fed him a good meal to build up his strength instead of asking why he was feeling weak and what he had smoked, swallowed, or drunk the night before.

Now he was about to come off the starting line with thirty other high-powered motorcycles roaring around him. If he didn't have the strength he needed or all his wits about him, his life could be in danger. My hands began to sweat as I stood watching the line of motorcycles, listening to the revving of the engines, which meant they would all be surging forward any second now. My gaze narrowed to single out my son. He was pitched forward on the bike, up over the handlebars. His head was cocked to one side, motionless, as he stared at the starter. His left hand held the clutch tight against the black rubber hand grip. It would take less than a fraction of a second for his gloved fingers to free the clutch and cause the powerful machine to leap forward. His right hand moved rapidly and continuously on the throttle.

The thirty-second sign was up, which meant the starter

could drop the gate whenever he wanted to, and seconds later he did. The loud roar of thirty motorcycles, all straining to be first as they came off the line, was accompanied by a huge cloud of dust that completely engulfed the riders and moved up the hill with the motorcycles, shutting out the spectators and making what happened inside very private, the rituals of an exclusive club. Still, they had those throttles wide open, each trying to be the first one into the first turn. They had to be hoping no riders fell in front of them, because if they did, there was no way to keep from running into them and going down also.

I held my breath, waiting for Jody to emerge from the dense dirt-filled haze. Finally I saw him—at the top of the hill, his white helmet just above the level of the dust. He was fourth from the front.

And now came the time for the cyclists to demonstrate their physical endurance. The expert riders had to race for thirty minutes (the other classes ran for only twenty), thirty minutes of grueling competition that would not only bring the best riders to the front but separate the physically fit and mentally alert from those who merely thought they were.

So far Jody was riding as well as I'd ever seen him ride. He'd worked his way up to second, and he and the rider running first were battling it out.

It was exciting, but it was also scary. He seemed to be taking too many chances. I wondered if the new bike was actually much better than last year's, or if he was performing for Lauren. That's it, I thought—Lauren. If he's a winner on the racetrack, he'll be a hero in her eyes. I was running from one end of the course to the other, as I always did, trying to see as much of the race as I could. Also, if he went down and was hurt, I wanted to be nearby to signal the medics or ambulance. I stopped at the snow fence beside the biggest jump. Lauren was there with some other girls. Jody and the boy in front were coming down the stretch toward us, both throttles held wide open. Good God, I thought, they're going into the jump without letting off on the gas at all. Jody was riding as if this was going to be his last race. His bike was gaining on the other one, outpulling the Yamaha. His new Suzuki must be some kind of racing bike, I thought, but, my Lord, they were going fast, too fast. The sound of the squealing engines flew past us as the two went into the jump. They were airborne, launched with full power. "Wow!" I said out loud. "Jody just passed him in mid-air."

I stood with my mouth open as Jody landed with a thud and took off, now in first place. The other boy landed just seconds behind him.

"Isn't he wonderful?" Lauren squealed with glee. "Wasn't that terrific?"

"I've never seen anything like it," I admitted. "But I think he's riding too fast for his first race. Do you know what kind of shock his arms just took coming off a jump like that? He's lucky he didn't rebreak his arm right then. I'm going over to the other side of the track. I'll see you a little later," I said.

I looked at the finish line. The flagman was showing the riders crossed flags. Half the race was over—God, fifteen minutes still to go. For the next ten minutes Jody and Greg Moores kept changing places. The end of the race was nearing, but Jody was really getting tired. I could tell by his expression when he passed that he was ready to put himself on automatic pilot and settle for second.

The next time he came around I ran to the side of the track and showed him four fingers and then doubled up both hands into fists, signaling that there were only four minutes left, and to hang on. He was shaking his head as if he wasn't sure he would be able to do it. Greg was now pulling ahead, putting some distance between himself and Jody and ensuring a first-place finish. He had it if he didn't fall. But second place was not that certain for Jody. Three other racers were moving up behind him.

The white flag was out—one lap to go. It seemed to rekindle Jody's drive and refuel his energies—only one lap. He wouldn't let anyone else pass him now, not with one lap to go. It seemed as if he mentally switched off the automatic pilot and kicked himself into overdrive. He was alive again, taking the turns tight, racing down the straightaways, and soaring over the jumps. The checker flag was out, and Jody took it standing up. He'd finished second, his first race of the year.

He did it, I thought, smiling to myself as I watched him ride off the track. He was sitting on the motorcycle now. His legs hung loose down the sides of the bike, almost dragging on the ground. His right hand was still on the throttle, but it was just resting there. The motorcycle was barely moving. His left arm was hanging at his side. He was beat. How in the world would he be able to race another thirty minutes today, to ride as hard as he had just done?

There are always two motos in moto-cross racing. The results of both races are tallied, and the winners for the day are determined by the best overall score. For example, a second and a fourth could beat a first and a sixth. Jody could win it all if he could repeat his performance.

I went to my car, got a big bottle of water out of the back and a couple of Cokes out of the cooler, and ran through the pit area to Jody's car. His motorcycle was resting against the trailer, and Jody was sitting on the ground beside it, leaning against one of the tires. Lauren and her girl friends, along with Eddie and Doug, were standing over him. Eddie and Doug were still in the B class, so they didn't race against Jody anymore.

"Why did you let Moores take first away from you, White? You some kind of wimp? You had it and you gave it to him." Eddie was giving Jody the normal postrace grief.

"Eddie Hanes, them's fighting words today," I said as I approached the group around Jody. "That was a heck of a race, and you know it."

"I'm just kidding him," Eddie said reluctantly. "But I still think he could have won if he'd really tried."

"Get out of here," I said, "or you and I are going to be rolling around on the ground." Eddie laughed and walked back to his trailer. I opened one of the Cokes and handed it to Jody. He took it and began to drink it without saying a word.

"You did a beautiful job, Jody. You scared me half to death, but it really was a magnificent bit of riding. And the way you hung on at the end! I don't know when I've ever admired you more. I know you really had to be hurting. How's your arm?"

"It aches, but I guess it's okay." Jody looked up as he spoke. His teeth, as well as his face, were covered with dirt. I handed him the bottle of water.

"Wash your mouth out before you swallow all that dirt." He swished the water around in his mouth and spat it out on the ground.

"Take your shirt off," I said. He held up his arms like a little boy who hasn't learned to do it for himself yet, and I pulled his racing jersey over his head.

"You want some water on your head?" I asked.

He nodded yes. I picked up the bottle of water and slowly poured it over Jody's hot, sweaty, and very dirty hair. The mixture of water and dust made mud as it ran down his face and onto his shoulders.

"Close your eyes," I ordered, and when he did, I splashed some water directly into his face. I saw a towel in the trunk of his car, got it, and handed it to him. We wiped away some of the water and dirt.

"Feel a little better now?" I asked.

"A little."

I kneeled down in front of him.

"Jody, I think you ought to consider *not* racing in the second moto. Why don't we just call it a day right now and chalk it up as preparation for the rest of the year?"

He looked as though I had asked him to commit treason against his country or, worse yet, abandon his dream.

"Maaah-om, and throw away that second I just worked so hard to get? If I do anything at all in the next race, I could win. I could start off the season listed at the top, or near the top, of the expert class."

For five years that had been his goal: someday to be the top on the 125 expert class. There was no doubt he had the ability to achieve it, but I thought it could wait another week or two or another couple of months, maybe even a year. The mother in me prevailed.

"Jody, that can wait. You're just getting over a broken arm and sprained leg. You need to build up your strength and endurance. If you push yourself today, you may get hurt and be out the rest of the year. You rode a great race. Just be content that you *can* beat these guys—all of them. And the bike is beautiful. Boy, when you turned it on, it responded."

"I know. It's the best motorcycle I've ever had. I'll be all right, Mom. A couple hours of rest and I'll be ready to ride."

"I'm afraid in a couple of hours you'll stiffen up and be in worse shape than you would be if you went out there right now."

"Mom, I'm going to race in the second moto."

It seemed to be something that he wanted to do so badly I couldn't say no.

"Okay. Well, I'm going to get you some lunch, then. I'll be back."

"Would you take my boots off first?" he asked.

"Sure."

I unbuckled his racing boots and pulled them off. He unbuckled his leather racing pants, and I knew he wanted me to pull them off also. The jeans underneath were soaking wet with perspiration. Jody held out his left hand, not his painfully sore right one. I took hold of it and pulled him to his feet. He put his arm around Lauren, who had been standing there watching all this time, saying nothing. They went to sit in the car, and I went to get Jody something to eat. And he's going to race again today, I thought. He may ride, but he won't be racing.

Jack and Christopher got to the track shortly before Jody's second moto was about to start. I explained how well the first race had gone and how nervous I was about this one.

I folded my arms on top of the snow fence and leaned my chin on them as I once again looked down the hill at the motorcycles and riders on the starting line. They lined up according to where they had finished in the first race. Jody and Greg Moores had the two best positions, on either side of the center pole but right in the middle of the pack, so if anything went wrong, they'd be mowed down. I took a deep breath and let it out quickly in an effort to relieve the tension I was feeling.

"Please, dear God, make him be all right," I prayed silently. "I don't care how he does in the race. I just want him to live through it."

The gate went down, and the noise and dust surged up the hill. I stood motionless and stared at the spot where I knew I'd be able to see the first one to come out of that mess. It was Jody. My God, it was Jody—Jody and Greg, right together.

"It's Jody," I screamed at Jack. I was jumping up and down and pounding on his shoulders. "It's Jody, it's Jody. He's first. I can't believe it. He's in front."

"Take it easy. He's got a long race ahead of him. Don't get so excited yet," Jack warned.

He was right, and it didn't take long for Jody's abused body to start showing signs that it would never last through *this* race, at least not at the peak level of performance it would take to stay in front. One lap, and Greg had passed him. Two laps, and two other riders had overtaken him.

The front four roared over the hill and down onto the back side of the track, out of our view. The rest of the racers followed close behind, looking and sounding like bees funneling into a hive. My eyes shifted to where they would come out of the woods and back into sight. I stared at the empty track and listened to the muffled sounds of the machines echoing in the distance.

Two motorcycles leaped into view. One of them was Jody's.

"Jody's second," I said to Jack, surprised. "Something must have happened to Greg and the boy who was second. They must have gone down in the woods."

A flagman also noticed the change and ran over the hill to see if the missing riders were hurt or if they had fallen on the track and he would need to put out a yellow flag. That would warn the other riders of trouble ahead.

Jody and the front-runner were racing into a sharp U-turn. Jody was going to try to take him on the inside. I dug my nails into the palms of my hands. He was going too fast for a turn that sharp. The bike was almost perpendicular to the track. His right leg was down on the ground, providing a pivot point.

"That injured leg can't take that weight or strain," I mentally warned Jody.

He accelerated too quickly and the motorcycle skidded out from under him.

"Oh, no, he lost it!" I said out loud.

Jody hit the track and lay in the dirt, practically in the middle of the track. Motorcycles were flying over him, skidding around him. One even jumped off the course to avoid hitting him.

"Put the yellow flag out," I screamed. "Get up, Jody. Move out of the way," I yelled.

Jody scurried off the track as if he'd heard me. He appeared to be all right, but he wouldn't be able to get to his motorcycle until all the riders got by it.

"Well, there goes that race," I said. "He ought to push that bike back to the pits right now."

But just as I finished saying that, Jody rushed to the middle of the track, picked up the bike, hit the kick starter, and headed out after the pack, dead last.

He was really flying now.

"That kid amazes me sometimes," I said to Jack. "When a lot of riders would give up, that's when he rides his heart out."

225

Before one lap had been completed Jody had passed half the riders and was back in the middle of the pack. I was jumping up and down and cheering him on. It was exciting and inspiring.

But as the group of motorcycles all roared into the Big Berm turn, several riders went wide, forcing Jody off the track. He was going too fast and his strength was fading. He went down again. All the motorcycles he had just worked so hard to pass sped past him. He struggled to get his bike up again, but he could barely lift it. The tires of the other motorcycles were kicking dirt into his face as they raced around the turn, once more leaving him behind.

I wanted to cover my eyes. It hurt to watch the agony of my son's struggle to go on. I wanted to run down on the track and help him, but I knew I couldn't. I stood there helpless, watching as he finally righted the bike, got on it, and started out again.

Jody held the throttle wide open as he took off down the track. He went over a jump all alone. The motorcycle flew through the air. He was leaning too far forward, and the bike came down on the front tire instead of the back. I gasped and threw my hands up to my mouth. The motorcycle was going to flip. Jody tried to pull back on the handlebars and shift his weight to the rear, but it was too late. Seconds later he was once again sprawled on the ground.

"That's it. I can't take anymore. He's going to kill himself," I said. I frantically squeezed through an opening in the snow fence and raced across the infield to where my son lay in a heap, his twisted motorcycle beside him.

"Jody," I screamed, "are you all right?"

He was getting up. "Yeah."

"You're not going out there again. You can't race anymore. You don't have the strength. Do you hear me?"

Jody was pulling his bike off the track and out of the way of the other riders.

"I've got to finish, Mom. I'll get points for this race no matter where I finish."

"You can't," I said, standing with him. "Look at your motorcycle. The handlebars are bent."

He stood in front of the bike and put the front tire between his legs to hold it still while he jerked on the handlebars to straighten them. The fender was broken, but that wouldn't keep it from running or stop Jody from riding it.

"Jody, I don't want you to go back out there. You're exhausted. It's too dangerous. You're going to kill yourself, and I'm not going to stand here and watch it."

A strange expression swept over his face, one I'd never seen before. I felt as if I knew something I wasn't supposed to know, as if I were reading his mind. It sent a chill through my hot, sweaty body. He quickly turned away, shutting me out. I was left staring at the back of his head, wondering what that look had meant. I shivered as if to shake off the strangeness and the chill I was feeling.

"Come on. Let's get this bike back to the pits and call it a day," I urged. The roar of the motorcycles coming around again to complete another lap was getting louder. I guess Jody figured he'd lost so much time by now he might as well hang it up. He got on the battered bike, kick-started it, and slowly rode across the infield of the track. I followed on foot. He looked so dejected. Maybe I shouldn't have insisted that he quit. Maybe I should have let him go on racing and just told him to take it easy.

Lauren and the girls gave Jody a little cheer as he rode off the track. He hardly looked up. Well, at least he's in one piece, I thought. There will be lots of other races. But he needs to get himself in shape if he intends to do any serious competing, I told myself, with the intention of telling Jody. The most superb ability and strongest will to win cannot override a poor physical condition, at least not consistently in a sport as demanding as moto-cross.

Back at Jody's car I found his motorcycle lying on the ground, where he had dropped it in disgust. His helmet had been thrown down next to it. He was lying on the front seat of his car with his legs dangling out the open door.

"It's not the motorcycle's fault, you know," I said with considerable irritation at his childish behavior. "That motorcycle cost a lot of money, and that's no way to treat it, no matter how upset you are."

He sat up. "You're going to take it home," he dictated in a very unpleasant tone. I decided to ignore his abrasiveness, feeling it was coming from anger and exhaustion. It was totally out of character for Jody, so I thought it was probably best not to make a big deal about it.

"I'll take the motorcycle home," I said calmly. "I'll go get my car right now. We'll put the trailer on it, load up the bike, and I'll be gone. What are you going to do?" I asked.

"I'm going to take Lauren home," he said, "and I don't want to be dragging the trailer and motorcycle along with me."

"Okay," I said continuing to keep cool. "I'll go and get the car right now."

"Bring me a couple of Cokes too," he ordered.

I walked away without responding, but he knew I'd heard him, and he probably knew I didn't like what I'd heard.

Why was Jody behaving this way? Was he angry because I had told him not to finish the race? Was he angry because he'd listened to me rather than do what he wanted to do? Did he feel I'd made him look like Mama's boy in front of Lauren and his racing buddies? Was he asserting himself now because he had gone down on the track? He was ordering me around as his father used to do, telling me what I was going to do rather than asking me nicely, demanding things without a please or a thank-you. Was that it? Was he taking on the role of his father to try to show me he was grown up and didn't need my advice or want me to impose my wishes on him? Did he think acting like this made him more of a man?

I wanted to shake my son and tell him that that was no way to behave, that he shouldn't be treating me that way just because I was concerned about his life, just because I didn't want him to get seriously hurt. I wanted to say, "You're racing because you want to. I buy you motorcycles and come to the races because I know it's something you want me to do. You're not racing to please me, and if you want to race, you can certainly take your bike home afterward. It's not my job to put your toys away."

But I didn't say any of that. I made more excuses for him. He was physically wiped out. He was mentally and emotionally distraught by his failure to do well in the last race. He had screwed up the opportunity to impress Lauren, and it was easy to blame me. I understood that, and I could take it. As always, if it lightened my son's burden, I accepted it gladly.

I also think Jody was missing his father on that day, remembering the good times they had had racing motorcycles and forgetting the bad, forgetting the times John pushed Jody when he didn't want to be pushed, the times he told him he hadn't tried hard enough. John wouldn't have encouraged him to come off the track. He would have given him hell for falling, for riding so poorly, and for being out of shape. I think Jody had been able to forget that side of John in the two and a half years since his father's death. I think only the good memories lingered, which caused a longing in my son, a longing for the good times shared by a father and a son—those wonderful times at the motorcycle races and at the motorcycle club events. They would get up early on weekends and come home late. Sometimes they'd be covered with mud from riding in the woods and streams. They'd be arm in arm, dog-tired but happy, full of their day's adventures and misadventures.

Many times Marjorie and O'Donnell would also go to the events, and so did I before John and I were divorced. But for Jody it meant more. It was his special time with his dad. It was that side of his father that he wanted to imitate. It was the part of his father that he loved and admired, the part that always had time for him, the part that had unending patience when it came to fixing and rebuilding a bike, the part that would show and teach and praise as well as criticize. It must really be hard to lose that kind of close paternal companionship. Jody had probably asked himself a hundred times why their relationship hadn't been enough to keep his dad alive. It had meant so much to Jody; why hadn't it been enough for his father? Jody must have felt he had failed his father somehow. Why else would he have killed himself and left Jody behind?

There is the possibility that during the times he missed his father, along with blaming himself, Jody also blamed me for that missing relationship, and perhaps he even resented me for not being able to fill his father's shoes.

The week following that race, which was the last race my son would ever ride, I harped on a fitness program to get him back into shape. Good food, exercise, lots of sleep—"good clean living," I had said, so he would get the message that he should give up drugs. It was my cowardly way of including that without bringing up the subject I didn't know how to handle and Jody didn't want to talk about. I ask myself now how I could have avoided talking about something that was changing my child and threatening his life.

Jody listened to my fitness plan, but he didn't pay much attention. He had other things on his mind. I think he was having problems with Lauren again, but he didn't want to talk about them. He wouldn't even talk about the motorcycle race. When I tried to discuss it he just said, "Forget it, Mom, it's over, just forget it. It doesn't matter."

A week of going through the motions for Jody led into a tiring and emotionally draining weekend. I didn't know how draining or disturbing until Monday.

CHAPTER 11

IT CAN'T HAPPEN
❧
MAY 9, 1977

"**A**RE you feeling any better today?" I asked Jody as he walked into the kitchen to have breakfast before going to school.

"Yeah, I'm okay."

"You sure weren't okay yesterday."

"I'm okay today."

"Well, I've got a nice breakfast for you, a good way to start off a Monday."

"Mom, I'm really not very hungry, and I have some homework I have to finish after I get to school. I'll just have some orange juice."

"Why didn't you do all your homework over the weekend? You know you shouldn't wait until Monday morning to finish it."

"I forgot to bring home the book I needed."

"It seems you're forgetting an awful lot of things these days."

"Mom, I've got to go." Jody got up to leave.

"Well, here, take this English muffin with you." I shoved it into his hand before he could say no. With the muffin squeezed in his hand, he lifted his schoolbooks off the dining room chair.

"Do you have money for lunch?"

"I think so," he answered.

"Wait a minute," I said. "I'll get you some so you'll be sure."

I ran into the den, grabbed a five-dollar bill out of my pocketbook, and stuffed it into his back pocket as he was going out the door. "There's a little extra there in case you need gas."

"Thanks, Mom."

"I'll be home for dinner tonight. I'll bring something good home. What would you like?" I asked as I followed him out to his car.

"I don't know," he answered in his usual way when asked about food.

"Well, I'll get something special, a steak or something. I haven't seen much of you this past week. Either you've been out or I've been out. Maybe I ought to make a date to see my son," I teased.

He opened the door to his car, threw his books onto the passenger seat, put the English muffin in his mouth, wiped his hand on his jeans, got in, and started up the car. He took a bite out of the muffin as he pulled it from his mouth.

"Bye, Mom," he said through a mouthful of muffin.

"Bye, darling. Have a good day, and drive carefully."

If he said "I will," I didn't hear him, because the car was already headed down the driveway. I stood staring after him. He didn't look well, and his hair was too long and unkempt. He had washed it when he went out Saturday night, but not yesterday, and not this morning to go to school. Something was wrong. Something had happened over the weekend. He had been out late both Friday and Saturday nights, and he had spent most of Sunday in bed. But there was something even more disturbing. On Sunday I was doing the yearly job of cleaning out the pool when I started to get upset about not having any help on this project. I started talking to myself about how I was sure everyone would come around when the job was finished to swim in the pool. But had I asked for help? No. "So, Susan," I said, "you have no reason to complain." With that, I got out of the pool and went to the third floor to get Jody up to help.

It was about one o'clock in the afternoon, and he was still sound asleep. He hadn't come in until almost five that morning—which was the latest he had ever stayed out. I put my hand on his shoulder and shook him gently.

"Jody, it's time to get up. I need your help for cleaning out the pool."

His eyes opened, but he looked as if he didn't know where he was.

"Hi, it's me. It's after one o'clock, and I've got a wonderful job for you—helping me clean out the pool. It's a beautiful day, really sunny, and you can get a great tan out there."

He looked at the clock. "I'll be down in a few minutes," he promised.

"Okay, but don't be long. You're missing the opportunity of a lifetime to get a summer suntan in May. It's actually hot down in the concrete bowl of that pool today."

"I'll be out."

It was almost an hour later when Jody stumbled out to

the pool. He was wearing his cut-off jeans and no shirt. He was dressed to work and to get that tan, but he looked ghastly—weak and shaky—and I knew I wouldn't get much help from him that day.

"I've gotten most of the leaves and crud out of the bottom, but I need the sides scrubbed," I said, handing Jody a brush and a bucket of acid solution.

He put his left hand on the rim around the top of the pool and, with the brush in his right hand, he bent over to scrub the side. After a few strokes he appeared to get dizzy. He dropped the brush and stood up. When he had steadied himself, he went to the shallow end of the pool and sat down.

"What's wrong?" I asked.

"I don't feel so good. I'll be all right in a minute." Jody lay back on the hot concrete. The sun beat down on his upturned face and outstretched body. His arms and legs seemed limp, and perspiration popped out on his face, running back into his hair.

I knew he had a terrible hangover from something. Realizing it was probably drugs rather than liquor, I began to feel nauseated myself. He looked so weak and pathetic. I went inside to get him a cold Coke, resolved to find some way to stop his self-destructive behavior. I was taking the bottle cap off when I heard him coming in the back door.

"I'm going back to bed, Mom. I really feel sick, and the sun's just making it worse."

For a second my concern for my child turned to anger at what he was doing to himself and his lack of concern for my needs and wishes.

"You act as if you don't have a care in the world. Don't

you feel any sense of responsibility to help out around here anymore? All you think about is staying out late and partying. There's more to life than that, you know."

His head jerked around, and he shot me a look I'll never forget. It was an expression that reflected shock, pain, and disappointment at my apparent lack of understanding of what he was feeling or going through. But he said nothing. He just stared at me with that same expression as if he were seeing or hearing something he couldn't believe. Finally his eyelids dropped and his head rolled forward until his chin came to rest on his chest. He turned, walked out of the kitchen, and went upstairs and back to bed.

Guilt and regret surged through me the minute I saw that look on my son's face. How could I have said those things to him? How could I have been so insensitive? I rushed up to his room with the Coke in my hand. I kneeled down beside his bed.

"Forgive me, Jody. I didn't mean what I just said. I just hate seeing you like this. I want you to feel good and be strong and alert. I want you to do things and have the strength to do them. I brought you a Coke, and I'm going to fix you something to eat. You'll feel better after you've eaten something."

As I look back, I realize there was something terribly important missing from almost every conversation I ever had with Jody. I told him what I wanted—for him and from him. Rarely did I give him the chance to tell me what he wanted. Did he really want to go on racing motorcycles? I assumed he did because it had been so important to him while his father was alive. I believed it still was. I had been so determined that nothing would change after John's death that in a way I stifled Jody's growth and expansion into new areas.

For example, I didn't ask if he wanted to go to college. I assumed he would go. I would have thought that if he didn't, it would be a terrible waste of a wonderful mind. But what did Jody want to do? I didn't ask.

Jody stayed in his room all day and all night. I took him a sandwich, and later I took dinner up to him. Except for eating the meals, he slept.

The next day, a warm, cheerful Monday morning in May, I convinced myself that Jody was feeling better. After all, he was going to school. If he didn't feel well, he could have said he was going to stay home sick. But he *was* going to school, and he was concerned about getting his homework finished. I listened as his car turned off the dirt lane and onto the paved road. I could hear the gears shifting as he accelerated. Not too fast, Jody, I thought, take it easy. One ticket's enough. I went back inside to get ready to go to work.

Marjorie was up and in the kitchen. She had gotten home from college on Saturday, her classes finished for the year. It was good to have her around again. Marjorie had turned twenty-one in March, and although she was busy with her own life and her relationship with her boyfriend Jody Westerlund, it was good to have her running in and out of the house. I always felt better when all the children were home, and I was eagerly awaiting O'Donnell's return from her college in Boston. I was really looking forward to a summer with everyone around. Jack and I were planning to rent the beach house in Ocean City again in August. Maybe it would work out that we could all be there together again.

"Hello, and how are *you* this morning?" I asked as I greeted Marjorie.

"I'm fine."

"What are your plans for the day?"

"Nothing much, just hanging around here."

"Will you be home for dinner?"

"I think so."

"Good. I'm going to get a steak or something special. We'll have a really good dinner, just the three of us."

"What's the occasion?"

"Nothing really. Just that we're all three going to be home. I was out several nights last week—working late, making a public appearance, or going out with Jack. Poor Jody was here alone or over at Eddie's or maybe at Lauren's every night."

"Probably Eddie's," Marjorie commented. "I don't think things are going very well with Lauren."

"What makes you say that? She was with him at the races last weekend."

"Oh, just the look on his face when I asked how his girl friend was. He just kind of shrugged his shoulders, but he didn't look very happy."

"Well, tonight's *our* night—no boyfriends or girl friends, just us. I've got to get dressed or I'm going to be late for work. I'll see you tonight."

"Okay, Mom. Have a good day."

"You too, honey."

That evening I was pacing around the newsroom, anxious to get home, but I knew I had to stay on the news set for the seven o'clock broadcast. The anchor desk was set up in front of the reporters' desks, so that the evening news could be read from a real newsroom and not just a set. It was supposed to give our news more credibility than the other two stations in town had, where the anchors read from studio sets. It was one of those gimmicks dreamed up by a consultant to attract viewers and increase the ratings. Even though the reporters had long since finished writing and editing their reports for that night, we were required to sit at our desks on the set and look busy. We were very expensive props.

The lights had gone on over the anchor desk. The anchors, sports, and weather men were in place, and I was getting ready to sit in my chair when the phone on my desk rang.

"Susan White," I said cheerfully.

"Mom." It was Marjorie and something in her voice frightened me. She paused. "Mom," she continued, "this is an emergency." She was warning me that something awful had happened. "Mom"—this time screaming into the phone, panic taking over her voice—"Jody's shot himself."

"You're kidding," I yelled into the phone, knowing she wasn't but desperately hoping she was, my mind refusing to accept what she said.

"No, Mom, I wouldn't kid about this. It's because of Lauren. He left a note. It says he loved her too much. What am I going to do?" she wailed. "I've called the fire department."

"Is he still alive?"

"Yes."

"Just hold on, Marjorie. I'll get the helicopter there. They'll fly him to Shock Trauma. Try to stay calm. I'm going to hang up now."

I put the phone down and screamed at the top of my voice, "No, no, no, they can't do this to me. Not my Jody. They can't take my Jody from me. This can't happen to me."

Everyone was staring at me.

"It's Jody. He's shot himself, just like his father." Tears flooded my face as I screamed out my agony. I ran from the studio newsroom to the assignment room on the other side of the soundproof door. It hadn't kept my screams from being heard. People were coming from every part of the building to see who was screaming and why. Inside the studio they were somehow beginning the newscast. I could see and hear anchorman George Rogers on the TV monitor behind the nighttime assignment editor, Karen Walker.

"What is it, Susan? What's wrong?" Karen pleaded for an explanation.

"It's Jody. Jody's shot himself. We've got to get the med-evac helicopter to him. Please call, please hurry."

I sobbed as I heard the words come out of my mouth. "Oh, Jody, no. You couldn't do this to me. You know how much I love you. You are my life." I dropped to my knees, putting my hands and my head on the top of Karen's desk. I listened as she tried to convince the State Police dispatcher to send the helicopter to get Jody.

"It's Susan White's son. He's, ah, he's, ah, he's been shot."

Karen took the phone away from her ear. "They can't send the med-evac helicopter out until someone official, on the scene, has confirmed that it's really needed."

"That'll be too late," I screamed as I jumped up and grabbed the phone from her.

"Hello, this is Susan White," I cried out into the phone. "My son has shot himself. My daughter is with him. For God's sake, send the helicopter now. It may be the only chance we have of saving his life. Please!" I cried. "Please send it." I started to sob uncontrollably.

"It's on the way, Mrs. White. Hang on and I'll get the

exact location from you." The calm voice of the State Policeman came back into my ear. "Now tell me exactly where your house is, Mrs. White, and where the closest field is for the helicopter to land in."

I gave him the location and explained that we lived on a farm and that there was a field fifty feet from my front door. When I had finished giving directions I hung up and called Marjorie. One quick ring and the phone was snatched up.

"Hello."

She was with Jody in his room, right next to the phone.

"Marjorie, the helicopter is on the way. It should be there in a few minutes." I was almost afraid to ask. "Is Jody still breathing?"

"Yes, I think so. I made sure his tongue wasn't down his throat."

"You've done everything right, darling. Maybe he'll be all right."

"That's what I keep thinking, Mom. He used the old 22 rifle. I keep hoping the bullet just hit some bone in his head and he'll be fine."

It was an old, almost antique rifle. I don't know where he had found bullets for it.

"Pray, darling. We've just got to pray he'll pull through." I heard voices. "Who's there with you?" I asked.

"The ambulance crew from the Gamber Fire Department and Louis from down the road."

"Ask Louis if he can bring you to the hospital. I don't want you driving."

"He's going to. I already asked him," she said, a good deal calmer now.

She really must believe Jody will be all right, I thought. That calmed me down and gave me hope.

"I hear the helicopter, Mom. I've got to go now. I'll see you at the hospital. He'll be all right. He's got to be."

"I hope so, darling." I hung up and began to cry again.

I didn't know it but Karen had called Jack at his apartment to tell him what had happened. He got to the station a few minutes later, and I turned around as he walked through the door.

"Jody's shot himself, just like John," I blurted out, the tears and words seeming to run together. "I should have listened to you and gotten rid of all those guns."

Jack took me in his arms. "I can't believe he would do it," he said.

"Neither can I, not Jody, not my Jody."

I put my head on his shoulder and sobbed out loud. Jack held me tight and let me cry, stroking my head, a caring touch that said more than words.

"The med-evac helicopter is out at Susan's now picking him up," I heard Karen telling Jack. "She got it there. Why don't you take a news car and drive Susan down to Shock Trauma? If I hear anything, I'll call you on the two-way radio. Here, take R-17." She handed Jack the keys. With an arm still around me he guided me toward the door. "Let's go to the hospital so we'll be there when Jody gets there."

I nodded my head in agreement and went on crying. We drove quietly downtown through the familiar city streets, listening to the sounds coming from the police and fire radios and from our news radio as Karen dispatched news crews to cover stories as if it were just another routine night.

"KDV346 to Jack and Susan."

Jack picked up the radio mike. "Go ahead, Karen."

"I just got a call from the State Police. The helicopter

is on the way. It should get to University Hospital in about five minutes."

"Thank you," Jack said and put the mike back on its hook.

I looked up over the Baltimore skyline and saw a helicopter in the distance approaching the city from the west.

"There it is," I said. "Hurry." Jack stepped on the gas.

My son's in that helicopter, I thought, possibly dying. It all seemed so unreal. Yet I'd been through it before, driving to this same hospital for the same reason two and a half years ago. It seemed like yesterday. But John was different. John was forty-three years old. Jody's only seventeen, I thought. He's a baby. He's my baby. This can't be happening—it just can't. Jody will live. He just has to. Please, dear God, make him live, please. Dear God, don't take this precious child from me. Tears ran down onto my chest, soaking through my clothes. I could feel the dampness on my breast. I held that child to those breasts. He was such a good baby. He was my baby.

It couldn't end now. It couldn't end like this, with Jody following in his father's footsteps, following a man who didn't even want him to be born. He's my baby. I love him too much. This can't happen. When you love a child as much as I love Jody, it just can't happen!

Jack parked the car, and as we got out I could hear the helicopter hovering overhead getting ready to land on the roof of the hospital. We ran down the street and through the door that leads to the Shock Trauma unit. Oh, my God, I thought, it all looks too familiar: the sterile white walls, the red line on the floor leading through the automatic doors to the operating room.

One of the elevators had a red line leading away from it. That must be the elevator they'd use to bring Jody down from the roof. I stopped and put my hand out to stop Jack.

"He'll come down here," I said.

With that, the elevator doors opened. A stretcher was rolled rapidly out and down the hall toward us. Jody was on it, lying very still. There were tubes and bottles hanging from a pole extending above the stretcher.

"Don't try to stop us, miss," an attendant pushing the stretcher shouted roughly at me. I backed against the wall to let them pass.

I looked into Jody's face as he was rushed by me. His eyes were open and he appeared to be staring at the ceiling. His hair fell back from his face. I wanted to run after him. I wanted to take him in my arms to let him know I was there. I wanted him to know he wasn't alone in this strange, cold, sterile world. I felt if he knew I was with him, if he felt my hand in his, my arms around him, he would know I loved him and he would want to live.

The doors at the end of the hall magically opened, allowing the stretcher to roll through without even slowing down. The shiny metal doors then slid quietly back together, making my child disappear and shutting me out of his life, what was left of it. Jack's hands slipped into mine as he once again pulled me into his arms. Tears were now falling from his eyes.

"I didn't believe it until I just saw him. I didn't really believe he had done it," Jack whispered. Clinging to each other, we found our way to the waiting room, the same waiting room I'd been in before. It was all too horrible to be real—that this could be happening to us again.

When Marjorie arrived, her boyfriend, Jody Westerlund, who had gotten to the hospital ahead of her, was sitting with me holding my hand.

"It'll be all right. I'm sure it will be all right," he was saying.

When I saw Marjorie come into the room I jumped up and took her in my arms. We held each other for a long time and just cried. Then she explained what had happened.

"I was in the kitchen, Mom, when Jody came in. I asked him what he'd been up to. He said nothing, that he'd just been outside fooling around. Mom, he looked at me so strangely. I know he wanted me to say something to stop him. If I had only known what he was thinking, if I had only been more sensitive, if I hadn't been so involved in my own thoughts, if I had—" I cut her off.

"Marjorie, you couldn't have known. There's no way you could have sensed what he was about to do. You couldn't have known what to say."

I held my daughter as she sobbed in my arms. It was so unfair—first her father, now her brother. She loved them both and would have given her life to save them if she could, and now here she sat trying to figure out what she should have done to prevent this from happening, something over which she had no control.

"Jody went up to his room," Marjorie said, "and a little later I went upstairs to take a bath. When I came out of the bathroom I heard this noise coming from his room. It was Jody trying to breathe. I ran up and found him."

"Oh, my darling. How awful for you. How could Jody do this to us?"

"Mom, he didn't do it to us. He did it to himself. He was in such pain. He was so unhappy. He didn't think about what it would do to us."

We sat there waiting for someone to come and tell us

something. Meanwhile Charlie Horich, the head of the News Department, arrived. He is a big man with a heart to equal his size and a man who takes charge of every situation, even if he hasn't been asked to.

"Has anybody talked to you yet?" Charlie asked.

"I'm not sure anyone even knows we're here," I said.

Charlie left the room, and a few minutes later he returned with a doctor.

"Mrs. White," the doctor said. I stood up. "How long have you been here?" he asked.

"Since my son was brought in."

He seemed embarrassed. "We didn't know you were here."

"How's my son?"

"He's still alive, but he's lost a lot of blood. The paramedics did a wonderful job. They brought him back to life twice."

"Is there a chance that he'll pull through or are you telling me it's just a matter of time?"

Charlie jumped in: "I don't think Susan wants you to give her any false hopes. I think she wants to know if her son is going to die."

"I think it's just a matter of time," the doctor said matter-of-factly. "He's a strong young man and his body is continuing to function, but even if he lives, I don't know what shape his brain would be in. The bullet went in right behind the ear, passing through the most vital parts of the brain. He probably didn't feel any pain at all."

My legs buckled as I fell into the chair behind me. "Can I see my son—please, can I see him?"

"In just a little while. I'll send a nurse down."

The doctor left us to our pain and sorrow and tears. It

was happening. It really was happening. This awful thing was real. My Jody was really going to die.

About fifteen minutes later the doctor was back. "Mrs. White, I'm sorry. Your son has just died."

"I wanted to see him before he died. I wanted to hold him. I wanted him to know I was here," I cried.

"He wouldn't have been aware of your presence. I'm sorry, Mrs. White."

"I want to see him now. Can I please see him now?"

"The nurse will be down in a few minutes." He left again.

We hugged each other, and we cried.

O'Donnell—how would I tell O'Donnell? I couldn't tell her this over the phone. Charlie had called our minister, Philip Roulette, who had immediately come to the hospital. Phil volunteered to go to Boston to tell O'Donnell and bring her home. He would go by train because he didn't like to fly. He wanted to leave right then, from the hospital, but he didn't have enough money.

"I'll be right back," said Charlie. Half the News Department was waiting outside the Shock Trauma unit. Charlie went out and made them all empty their pockets onto the hospital floor. He gathered up the money and brought it back to Phil. I don't think they've been paid back to this day. Phil left, and I continued to wait to see my son.

Finally I couldn't sit still any longer. "Jack, I've got to do something. Let's walk down the hall."

Anger was rising inside me. For the moment it was overriding the grief. "He killed my baby, just as if he had taken the gun, put it to Jody's head, and pulled the trigger. John killed my son."

Jack let me express my anger. He let me rant and rave, and when my outburst had subsided, he held me as I returned to tears of grief and frustration. The anger wouldn't bring my son back. Nothing would.

When we got back to the waiting room a nurse was there.

"Do you still want to see your son?"

"Yes," I said. I looked at Marjorie.

"No. I don't want to, Mom. I'll stay here."

"I'm going with you, if that's all right," Jack said gently.

We stood beside the stretcher, looking down at Jody. He had a tube down his nose and throat, but other than that he looked as if he were asleep. The nurse had given me the silver cross he had been wearing around his neck, which had been a present from Lauren. The nurse had also given me his Poly school ring and a silver bracelet I had given him the past Christmas after he had told me boys wear bracelets now and it isn't considered effeminate. I was holding his jewelry tightly in my right hand. With my left hand I brushed the hair from his forehead.

"He never did get that haircut I was bugging him about," I said out loud. My tears poured onto the body of my son as I leaned down on him and hugged him as tightly as I could.

"Please, dear God, take care of him. Please, dear God, watch out for him. He's so shy, and he needs Your help. He can't make it on his own." I stood up and Jack put his arms around me to comfort me.

The nurse came to our side. "I think you'd better go now," she said with much kindness and concern. My fingers stroked his bare foot as we walked away. At the door I turned to look at Jody once more. He looked so alone lying there on the stretcher. He didn't like being alone. And yet I'd left him alone so much. I sobbed. Jack pulled me gently toward the door.

"Goodbye, Jody. I love you," I whispered.

My head ached so badly I thought it was going to explode. It was as if I were feeling the pain of Jody's bullet wound.

"I can't hold my head up," I said to the nurse. "I've got to lie down." She led me to a room with a bed.

"Can you give her something?" Jack asked.

"I'll get some aspirin." I took the aspirin and lay there with my eyes closed for a few minutes. Jack stood beside me stroking my head. I started thinking about Marjorie waiting downstairs.

"Let's go," I said. "We might as well go. It's not going to get any better."

Outside the hospital I stopped one last time and looked up at the lighted window of the room in which I knew Jody lay.

"I feel as if I'm abandoning my son," I said to Jack, giving in to a new flood of tears. "I don't want to leave him here. I want him back. I want another chance." I cried out in the night begging for a miracle. "I never thought this could happen to me. Please, someone, give me my Jody back."

My words were swallowed up in the darkness. No one could give Jody back to me, not now. It was too late. It was too late for that overdue talk with my son. It was too late to get help for his use of drugs. It was too late to get him counseling to help him deal with the death of his father and cope with his depression over losing his girl friend. It was too late to take a stand with my employer so that I could work nine to five and be home with Jody after school. It was too late for me, an adult, to show this teenager, my teenager, that his problems could be solved, that suicide was *not* an answer (in spite of the example his father had set for him), that by killing himself he was only destroying a very precious young life with great potential and leaving a great deal of incredible pain behind.

Jack and I stood on that dark, lonely street corner that night outside University Hospital holding each other, grieving and regretting. Our tears and thoughts ran together, prompted by what we didn't do, what we should have done, could have done, to prevent this tragedy. What a waste. What a terrible, terrible waste.

Eventually my thoughts turned to the living, the others who were sharing this pain.

"Lauren—I've got to go see Lauren," I said as I raised my head from Jack's shoulder. "I've got to talk to her. I can't let her take on the guilt for Jody's death."

"Tomorrow," Jack said. "Tomorrow we'll go to see Lauren."

CHAPTER 12

IT'S NOT YOUR FAULT

MAY 10, 1977

I AWOKE the next morning with a terrible empti-
ness, a feeling of deep despair. Jack
was lying beside me, and my daughter was in the next
room, but I felt all alone. My tears returned and so did
the lump in my throat. They would be my constant com-
panions now.

There would be great sadness for a long time, because
there had been such joy. Seventeen years of motherhood—
of love and caring, of worry and pain—would run through
my mind like a continuous picture show, and I would
know that similar scenes could never be repeated in real
life. I would never see Jody alive again. I would never
hear his voice, see him smile, or listen to him laugh. He
would never again sit on my bed and watch me put my
makeup on. He would never eat another Egg McWhite
or ride his motorcycle across the lawn, digging up the grass.

How in the world would I be able to bear this unbear-
able loss? The death of one's child is undoubtedly the most

difficult kind of death to deal with. But the death of your child by suicide is emotionally devastating. To know that your child chose to die in spite of your love and efforts to make life worthwhile for him can tear you apart.

You feel an incredible sense of failure. I knew that there was pain and turmoil in my son's life and that by turning his back on that agony, he wasn't specifically rejecting me. But the end result was the same. When Jody killed himself he ended our life together. He took with him a large part of me and left a void that was quickly filled with guilt.

My quiet tears turned to sobs, and Jack's arms slid around me to hold me and comfort me. He didn't say anything; he just held me. What could he possibly say? The time for words would come later.

When I had quieted down Jack got up, handed me a tissue, and turned on the TV. The local morning news was on, and I was looking at a familiar face. One of my friends in the business on another channel was talking about me as if I were a stranger.

"The seventeen-year-old son of Baltimore TV reporter Susan White was found shot to death in the family home last night. John O'Donnell White, Junior, was found in an upstairs bedroom with a bullet wound to the head. There was a 22-caliber rifle next to him. Police believe the wound was self-inflicted. An apparent suicide note was found next to the body of young John White."

Jack turned off the television. "I'm sorry," he said as he sat down beside me.

"That's all right," I said, accepting the fact that the public would know, should know, that my son had killed himself. Perhaps because of what I'd been through with John's death, I didn't want Jody's suicide covered up.

Even then I somehow knew it was best to be open about

my son's death. I didn't want to hush it up or say it was an accident, as so many family members of suicide victims do. I suppose I could have said he was cleaning the gun and it went off. But why? To avoid the shame some people think I should feel? I've felt intense grief, guilt, and regret but never shame.

The shame of suicide is that many people feel they can't deal with such deaths openly and honestly and don't seek the support and sympathy they need.

The shame and guilt that is often heaped on the families of suicide victims began for the most part in about the fifth century, when suicide was declared a mortal sin by the Roman Catholic church and, later, by the Anglican church. Taking one's life, the church councils decided, is an act inspired by the devil. The bodies of suicides were denied church burials, and, as a result, from the Middle Ages until as recently as the middle of the nineteenth century in Europe, when a suicide occurred, the body was degraded—spat on, and dragged through the streets to be jeered at by the townspeople. Many times the body was left unburied in the area reserved for public executions.

The last recorded incident of this type was in England in 1823. After that, Parliament passed a law ordering that the corpse of a suicide be buried privately in a churchyard or a private yard. But it wasn't until 1961 that a law was passed repealing the civil rulings about suicide, which had been based on the church doctrine. It wasn't until then that suicide was no longer designated a crime in England. It's no wonder that the families of suicide victims tried to cover up those deaths—tried to pass them off as accidents.

Suicide has never officially been considered a crime in the United States, but attempted suicide is a felony in nine states—though no one is known to have been charged or prosecuted for attempted suicide in those states. With or without criminal prosecution, the shame and stigma related to suicide remain in many communities today.

In 1969 Dr. Karl Menninger said, "The incidence of suicide will be reduced only when the public recognizes it as a psychological problem and as a medical problem, rather than as a moral problem and a disgrace to be covered up, regretted and forgotten. We have to stop whispering about suicide and talk about it out loud if we are ever to reverse the increasing numbers of people taking their own lives."

And right now the most urgent need for attention is in the area of teenage suicide. It's the second leading cause of death among teenagers. Suicide has become a horrible option for an increasing number of young people. The adolescent suicide rate is about 33 percent higher than that of the overall population. In 1983 about six thousand teens were known suicide victims. And this figure doesn't take into account the hundreds of young deaths written off as accidents but that may really have been suicides. It is estimated that every fourteen minutes in this country a teenager ends his or her life. If some disease were claiming the lives of our youth to that degree, there would be a national outcry that something must be done to stop it. Something should be done. Something can be done. Being open and acknowledging the problem is a beginning.

The TV newscast made me realize I hadn't called Jody's friends. Jack had called the family, mine and John's, but I was now afraid that others close to us would hear it on the news first. I wondered if Lauren even knew Jody was dead. I didn't know her number or where she lived. I didn't even know her parents' first names. Marjorie had told me that Jody had put her telephone number on the suicide note so we'd be sure to call her, but she couldn't remember what it was, and the police had taken the note. Eddie would know how I could reach her. I called, preparing myself to break the news to him and his family, just in case they hadn't heard. They had heard—on the radio. Eddie's mom, who had been like a second mother to Jody, began to cry as soon as she heard my voice.

"I know," she said, "but I can't believe it."

No one can believe that a young person can do such a thing. It's just too horrible and leaves us with a sense of helplessness. The hopes and dreams we hold for a child's bright, unexplored future are gone, and we're left with a feeling of disbelief that it all can be wiped out in a matter of seconds.

I called Lauren. She also knew. The police had been to see her as part of their investigation. I asked if I could see her, and she agreed. I remember thinking when we got to her house and she answered the door that she looked so young, younger even than fifteen. She was thin and frail-looking, and she was shaking as if she was very cold. I took her in my arms.

"It's not your fault, Lauren."

"I know," she said, trying to convince herself and apparently relieved that I didn't blame her.

"You can't be held responsible for what someone else does with his life."

"I know," she said again.

We sat at her dining room table.

"Did you have any idea that Jody was going to do this?" I asked as gently as I could.

"Yes. He said if I didn't go back with him, he was going to kill himself. But I didn't believe him. I didn't know what to do. He came over here yesterday and drove up and down in front of my house. Whenever I told him I wouldn't go out with him he'd come over here and park on the street to see if I went out with anyone else."

I couldn't believe what I was hearing. Jody had done the same thing to Lauren that John had done to me when I was fourteen. He couldn't have known his dad had done that. It sent a shiver down my spine.

"I didn't think you had been seeing each other for a while," I said. "I was surprised when he told me you were going to the races with him two weeks ago."

"We hadn't been, and I guess I shouldn't have started seeing him again. But I like, ah . . . liked Jody"—she corrected herself and started to cry. "I liked being with him, but I didn't want to be owned by him. He was so possessive. I told him Saturday night I wasn't going to see him anymore. He was really upset. He scared me, but I didn't know what to do."

"When did you last see him?"

"He drove over here after school yesterday. He just drove by the house for a while, and then he called me on the phone from his room. He said he was calling to say goodbye. He said he was going to shoot himself. I didn't know what to do."

"I wish you had called me. I wish you had told me the first time he ever mentioned suicide. But, then, you didn't know that he might really do it."

I didn't want to make her feel worse than she already felt. Jody must have had many ambivalent feelings before taking his life, and I think one selfish desire at the end was to make Lauren feel guilty. He wanted to do to her what his father had done to me. He wanted to punish her for making him miserable. He wanted her to be sorry she didn't go back with him. For some people suicide is the ultimate temper tantrum. With the self-destructive act they say, "If I can't have life my way, I won't have it at all, and you'll be sorry. You'll miss me when I'm gone." They think that by killing themselves they're showing the world how much they really loved someone. It's childish and it's futile. Lauren was sorry, but she was alive. Jody was dead.

I also think Jody wanted to be saved. He was crying out for help when he called Lauren. I think he not only wanted her to show she cared, he wanted her to try to stop him. I believe that when he hung up the phone he waited for her to call back and try to talk him out of it, and when she didn't, he felt he had no alternative but to go through with it. He must have felt total rejection; he must have believed that Lauren didn't really care if he lived or died, so he might as well be dead. At least he'd show her he meant what he said.

I've come to the conclusion that most teenagers who commit suicide really believe that no one cares if they live or die. I think they even believe that the people around them will be better off without them.

I loved my son more than I could ever put into words, and I was so sure he knew how much. Now I'm not so sure. I respected his intelligence and listened when he spoke. I never challenged his comments or opinions because I knew he was a person who spoke only from knowledge, not for the gratification of his own ego. I admired his brilliant mind, perfectly formed body, and sensitive soul, and I told him so. But I don't think I showed him how important he was to me by being there whenever he needed me! Whenever he was lonely, all the talk and gifts and professions of love couldn't make up for the reality that I chose to be elsewhere.

257

Time is more important than gold when it comes to saying I love you.

I think by the time he pulled the trigger on that gun he was convinced that no one really cared about his life. Sure, we'd be sorry for a while, but we had our own lives, and we'd get over it. I had Jack and my career, and he probably thought that by killing himself he would rid me of the one problem-filled burden in my life, himself. Depression can greatly cloud one's perspective, and I think Jody was seeing us all and his importance to us through a dense, pain-filled haze, further distorted by his use of drugs.

Before leaving Lauren I showed her the silver cross that was now hanging around my neck.

"Jody was wearing it when he died. I know you gave it to him, but I would like to keep it if you don't mind. It makes me feel better to have something that was important to him close to me right now."

The cross, which hung from a chain, lay close to my heart. I picked it up in my hand almost unconsciously, rubbing my fingers over its surface. Somehow it was a comfort to me.

"You keep the cross, Mrs. White, and I'll keep this Saint Christopher medal that Jody gave me."

She held up the small round medal on the long silver chain. It was the one I had given my son. All the children had Saint Christopher medals. It was a special talisman in our family. We would never go anywhere or do anything dangerous, such as riding motorcycles, without taking along "the protector." When Jody started racing motorcycles I always asked him before each race if he was wearing his Saint Christopher. I wondered how long ago Jody had given his medal to Lauren.

From Lauren's house Jack and I drove home to begin

facing hundreds of other questions that would never be answered and an empty house full of painful memories. Even the photographs or mementos that would ordinarily call forth smiles would now bring tears.

It began on the back porch, just inside the back door, where we hung up our coats and left our boots. We called it the mudroom for obvious reasons. Jody's jackets were on every other peg; his red-and-black wool jacket, his ski jacket, his down jacket, his denim jacket. His motorcycle boots stood together in the corner, his old ones and his new ones, his Bean boots and his ski boots. The bright red shelves on the wall next to the freezer held his hat and gloves, his motorcycle tools, and a half-empty can of motor oil.

Next I climbed the stairs to his room, the stairs that had taken me to Jody a thousand times over the past seventeen years. I had walked up them slowly when I wasn't anxious to face an uncomfortable situation. I had run up them in moments of happiness and excitement with news I couldn't wait to share with my son, and also during those times of fright when I needed to reassure myself that he was all right. No matter how I ascended that staircase to the third floor, it always took me to Jody. Today it would take me only to Jody's things. Each item I touched, each thing I looked at brought grief and pain. The bean-bag chair in the corner, where he had sat to shoot himself, the blood-stained carpet—my son's blood, shed for no good reason, shed because I was too caught up in my own world to prevent it.

Under Jody's bed was a wooden box that he had made himself. It was two feet long, a foot and a half wide, and four inches deep. I pulled it out, lifted the latches, and slowly opened the lid. I was almost afraid of the pain or secrets it might contain. I wasn't one to go through my children's belongings, and I felt as if I were snooping behind my son's back.

The box was divided into eleven sections, and each one contained some special treasure, something of importance to Jody, all neatly and carefully placed. My son was a perfectionist, and this box was further evidence of it: some cord coiled perfectly; a deck of cards stacked in sequence; keys and locks in their own little compartment; a Baltimore Clipper's hockey puck I had given him after doing a story on the team. There was a neatly folded Associated Press Photo Facts picture I had brought him. It pictured a lion at a zoo with his nose caught between the bars. I had written on the bottom of the picture "Things are tight all over." Jody had saved it.

Also folded carefully and in a section with other papers was an admission ticket to take the college boards. The date for the test was May 7, two days before he had killed himself. He hadn't used it. He must have already decided what he was going to do. He must have known there would be no reason to take the test to get into college. I hadn't even known the tests were being held on the seventh, or that Jody had signed up to take them. What else in my son's life hadn't I known about? I put everything carefully back in the box just the way I'd found it and closed the lid.

There was also a box under his desk that had a lock on it, but the lock had been pried open. Marjorie told me that the police had gone through everything in his room. I pulled the box with the broken lock out from under the desk. I lifted the lid. This was what I didn't want to see. This box contained bongs and cigarette papers and other drug paraphernalia.

"Oh, Jody, my poor Jody. What did I let you get into? I will never forgive myself for this."

I couldn't bear to look at the stuff. I put the lid back on the box. I would throw it in the garbage where it belonged.

On top of the desk was a copy of *The Little Prince,* by Antoine de Saint-Exupéry, in French. I figured Jody's French class at school must have been reading it. I had never read this children's classic, and I decided that when I got a chance, I'd get the English version, just to see what my son had been reading and studying right before his death.

Can you imagine my shock, months later, when I got the book and found that the little prince commits suicide? In a book written for children, the prince, a child from another planet, comes to earth. At the end of the book he makes an appointment with a yellow desert snake so he can return to his planet.

"You have good poison?" the boy asks the snake. "You are sure that it will not make me suffer too long?"

The conversation between boy and snake is overheard by an earth-born friend of the prince, who tries to stop him from keeping the appointment with the reptile. The little prince assures his friend that after the snake bites him he will only look dead, that he is leaving his body behind only because it is too heavy to take with him.

"But it will be like an old, abandoned shell," the little prince says. "There is nothing sad about old shells."

The book romanticizes suicide. The old shell is left behind, and the spirit is set free to soar to the heavens.

The Little Prince, I have found, was written a year before the author, a French aviator, flew off on a reconnaissance mission over France during World War II. He was never heard from again, and no trace of him was ever discovered. Suicide was suspected. Saint-Exupéry had written a letter and last will the night before he took off. He had also narrowly escaped in several mishaps, accidents that looked suspicious, and his other writings, in addition to *The Little Prince,* reveal a preoccupation with death.

I couldn't help wondering when I read it what influence this book and its author might have had on Jody's suicide. For one thing, John, Jody's father, was a private pilot. He killed himself. Saint-Exupéry, a pilot, was a suspected suicide, and he wrote in his fantasies that it might not be such a bad way to die. In fact, he said it might be quite pleasant. Was this just one more thing that encouraged my son to end his young life?

Jody's wallet was lying on top of his desk. I picked it up and looked through it. His driver's license: Class D and E, for driving a car and a motorcycle, issued 8/20/76, expiration date 3/8/78, his eighteenth birthday. That would never come, and the license would not be renewed.

There was a picture of Lauren, and a Baltimore City Public School's student ID card with an awful picture of Jody. He'd never showed me that, probably because of the picture. There were also insurance cards; his membership card for the American Motorcyclist Association; half a torn movie theater ticket; my signature on a scrap of paper. It looked like the bottom of some document. Why would Jody want that? To forge my name on excuse notes when he skipped school and I didn't know about it, I suggested to myself. I wondered how often that had happened. In the hidden billfold section was a crisp new two-dollar bill. It was the one I had given him in Ocean City when he beat me at wrestling.

It was all becoming so painfully clear to me now, now that it was too late. Jody liked wrestling with me because it was the only physical contact we had. It was hugging for us. Camouflaged by calling it wrestling, we were doing something we'd been taught not to do by Jody's father. We were physically displaying our affection for each other by touching and being close. By doing it under the guise of wrestling, Jody remained macho and I was simply being a tomboy all-American mother. How silly, when all we really wanted to do was reach out, hug each other and say, "I love you." How complicated we humans make life sometimes, how complex and destructive. Loving one's child should never be disguised as something else, not even as a game. When you play games, someone *always loses.*

I closed my eyes and remembered when I had come to Jody's room after our talk about his using drugs. I pictured where he was standing and how it felt when we hugged each other. I could feel his lean, muscular body in my arms. I could feel his strong arms, built up by motocross, wrapped tightly around me. I could feel my head resting against his.

I could feel the strength with which we held each other, how we clung together, not wanting to let go. I could feel it as if it was happening right then, and I longed to open my eyes and see my son. But I knew if I did, he wouldn't be there. He would never be there again, and I ached for my loss. I would never be able to hold Jody again, and I cried for all the times I could have and didn't.

I folded the wallet and held it in my hand. I would take it downstairs with me.

I opened the closet and looked at the clothes that he'd never wear again. Some he had never worn—the beige pants and vest. "I knew you wouldn't wear them when we bought them," I whispered. I closed the door, turned and looked around the room. Everything in this room meant something to Jody—the pictures pasted on the walls, most of which I'd snapped: Jody racing his motorcycle, Jody and his father, Jody and his friends.

Objects were scattered around the room—birthday presents and Christmas presents, all selected just for him, for his unique, special personality. *Things* that represented seventeen years of life—the Colts' pennant that was special because Jody had met quarterback Johnny Unitas. I had taken Jody with me to the Colts' training camp, and when Unitas came out on the field to practice, he waved to me. It was the one time in Jody's life that he was impressed with me, my position, or someone I knew. "Does *he* know *you?*" he asked. I proudly admitted he did, and thereby scored untold points with my son.

That person was gone now, and these *things* were all I had to hold on to. I couldn't look ahead to the future, because he wasn't in it. The past was all I had left. I had to look back. I loved him too much not to. Jody had to go on being a part of my life. I couldn't bear the thought of losing him altogether. The memory of my son would be the lifeline between us. I would spend many hours in my son's room, talking to him, crying, and trying to understand.

That search to know brought me sadness, almost too much to bear. Why hadn't I seen where he was headed? It seems to me now that he didn't have a chance.

First there was his father's suicide and the loss of any semblance of normal family life. Add to this my demanding career and deepening love affair, the loss of his school, the involvement with drugs, and his love problems that led to the loss of his girl friend. Jody's world was crumbling, and he must have felt he had no one to turn to, nowhere he really belonged. Every support system of Jody's had failed him, and I had failed, or refused, to see what was happening or to recognize its importance. My determination that our lives would be wonderful and problem-free just by my wishing and willing it so must have also walled up another outlet for Jody's problems and emotions.

The veil of sunshine that I wore in my effort to make everything okay for my son must have made him afraid to really talk to me. He probably thought I would be disappointed in him if he brought me his pain and problems. He might even have feared it would cause me also to reject him—a final rejection he wasn't going to risk. He would choose death over that.

The next two days were painful ones, but, I was to discover, not as painful as the weeks and months that lay ahead, the long and lonely hours of self-persecution.

The resentment would also build, resentment over the time I had spent with Jack and at my job when I could have been with Jody. I would even come to feel resentment over Jack's relationship with his son. What right did he have to share good times with Christopher when I no longer had my son? I'd listen to them laugh, and I'd weep for my Jody and begrudge them their happiness.

But in the hours after his death it was only grief I felt. And that was made easier to bear by the presence of many caring people. They came and went, all distraught and disturbed, all wondering how this could have happened to someone like Jody, someone so young. I found myself reaching out to try and comfort them, thus taking my mind off the depth of my sadness. Some came with words intended to make me feel better about Jody's suicide, but their words had the opposite effect. What they produced in me were feelings of frustration, even anger, because if I had known what these people had known, I might have saved my son.

One was a doctor who said, "It's not unusual for a teen-age boy to follow in his father's footsteps when the father has committed suicide. When an adult in a family kills himself, a child in that family is a good candidate to do the same thing, especially if the adult and child were close."

I stood staring at this well-meaning doctor in disbelief. I wanted to scream out my shock and indignation. Why hadn't he or someone else told me this when I could have done something about it? I had assumed that we all were less likely to commit suicide because John's death had made me so aware of the pain it caused the survivors. Why was he telling me this now when Jody was dead? The doctor knew that John had committed suicide, and he knew Jody was fourteen years old when it had happened, the most impressionable and vulnerable time in a teen's life. If someone, a professional, had said that to me right after John's death, I would have put Jody in counseling right away. I would have been on the lookout for danger signals, and I certainly wouldn't have dealt with his drug use and his depression over the loss of his girl friend as problems that would pass without help from a trained, knowledgeable person in the field of psychology or psychiatry.

Another shocking revelation came from a young, caring priest whom the kids and I adored. I was sitting at the kitchen table when he came in the back door. He took my hands in his and said, "Susan, I'm so sorry, but there may have been no other way for Jody. I picked him up after school once a week for eight weeks after his father's death, and he could never talk about it. We'd play chess, and he'd talk about his moto-cross racing, but any time I brought up his father, he changed the subject. Once he appeared to be on the verge of talking about it, but his eyes filled with tears and he stopped and went on to something else. It was just too painful for him to get out. He was so sensitive, perhaps too sensitive for this world."

I know this wonderful, loving man was trying to lessen my pain by making me feel that perhaps Jody's death was inevitable, was, perhaps, even for the best, that Jody's pain was over, that he was now at peace and that I should be too.

I hugged that priest and thanked him, but my mind raced with questions. Why hadn't I known that he had tried to help Jody for so many weeks after John's death? Was I such a terrible mother that I didn't even know what my children were doing? Why hadn't Jody told me? I guess it had been arranged between the priest and Jody, and since I didn't get home until eight o'clock each night, there was no way for me to know. But why hadn't the priest told me? He obviously had thought Jody needed some kind of counseling. When he saw it wasn't working with him, why hadn't he told me so I could get my son professional help?

After all, a priest is not a psychiatrist. Why had I been kept in the dark? Jody's death was not inevitable. No suicide is inevitable. I will never believe that. Something could have been done to save him. Something should have been done. The old myth that people who commit suicide are crazy—psychologically unbalanced from birth—and that if you prevent them from taking their lives sooner, they will eventually do it later is a lot of archaic baloney.

This is one of the many myths that exist about suicide. Psychiatrists tell us that the helplessness and depression

267

that lead to thoughts of suicide usually last only for limited periods of time. If the suicidal or depressed person can find proper treatment during that temporary period, he or she can eventually be helped to a full, productive, and enjoyable life. Professionals say that only a very few people who kill themselves or attempt to commit suicide can be labeled psychotic.

And then there were the three young girls who came with flowers in their hands. They looked as if they were on their way to a Sunday school play or a May Day celebration—three beautiful teenagers, as fresh as the flowers they carried, with shiny hair and bright, clear eyes. But instead of the carefree smiles you would expect to see on the faces of such lovely children, their eyes brimmed with tears. I had never seen them before, but my heart went out to them. I knew they must have known Jody and cared about him.

"Hello, Mrs. White, I'm June, and this is Cindy and this is Kathy. We knew Jody." That was all I needed to hear. I hugged them all as tightly as I could. We cried together as if we had known one another for years. We shared a sadness that bound us. I took the flowers and led them inside. When we had dried our eyes and blown our noses, we talked.

June told me how they had gotten to know Jody at various parties and that she had wanted to go out with him. In fact, they all had, but Jody wanted only Lauren.

"Once," June said, "when Jody and Lauren had broken up, he was at my house for a party. He had come with Eddie and some of the other guys. Jody wouldn't come downstairs to where the party was. He just sat upstairs in the den and moped. I tried to talk to him. I told him that Cindy or Kathy would love to be his date and go out with him sometime, but he didn't want anything to do with them. He just wanted to talk about Lauren. I told him he was ignorant to be depressed over Lauren, that she wasn't worth it. But he said he loved her and he would never love anyone else. He said he was going to kill himself, just like his father did."

"He did?" I asked with shock. "What did you say?"

"I said he was crazy and not to talk like that. I didn't think he meant it."

"How long ago was that?" I asked.

"About a month."

Oh, my God, I thought to myself, he'd been thinking about it for that long, maybe even longer.

"I wish you had called me and told me," I said as gently as I could. I didn't want it to sound like a reprimand, and I didn't want June to think she was to blame for not telling me my son was talking about suicide.

"I didn't think he meant it," she repeated. "I thought he was just trying to scare me or make me feel sorry for him because Lauren wouldn't go back with him."

"I understand," I said as I held her hand and tried to comfort this bewildered teenager who was having as much trouble coping with the realization of Jody's death as the rest of us were.

What June didn't know at the time, nor did I, is that Jody was probably asking for help when he talked about killing himself. He didn't know how to handle those self-destructive feelings, and he didn't know how to get help from someone who did. Another myth about suicide is that people who talk about killing themselves never do. We must take all such threats seriously. And if a friend says he or she is thinking about suicide, never say "You're crazy, don't talk like that. I don't want to hear it." It makes that person, especially a young person, think he really is crazy for thinking such thoughts, and he will avoid any further conversation about it. He will, once again, withdraw into himself, hiding his thoughts from others who might be able to help.

We must encourage someone who has opened up about suicidal thoughts to talk about them by asking "Why?" and "How?" And if that person has a plan, a method, a definite time and place all thought out, he is serious and needs help immediately.

Don't be afraid of betraying a friend's confidence. Such a "betrayal" could save his life. Call family members or friends of that person and let them know that suicide is on the mind of someone they love. Give them the chance to do something about it. If they don't know, they can't help.

CHAPTER 13

GOODBYE, JODY

MAY 12, 1977

*I*T HAD all led to this moment, I thought, staring at the coffin that held the body of my son. It wasn't any single thing that had caused him to end his life but a lot of things put together. We had all failed him at some crucial period along the way.

I looked once again at the people huddled together to say goodbye to Jody—and maybe to ask his forgiveness.

I looked down at Lauren, who stood beside me sobbing openly. I put my arm around her to try to comfort her. She would have to deal with this the rest of her life. Every relationship she entered into would be affected by Jody's suicide. I ached for her as I thought of her future. I drew her closer to me to let her know I cared. She wailed with grief and guilt.

Jack stood beside me, his head bowed. He occasionally looked over at Christopher, who was standing next to his mother, Jack's former wife. Christopher held on tightly to her hand for reassurance and security. Jody had been the closest thing to a brother Christopher had ever known. He looked up to him, he respected him. What effect would Jody's death have on him? What example had been set for him?

There was sadness mixed with determination in Jack's face. This wouldn't happen to his son. He wouldn't make the same mistakes I had made. He had learned from my painful lesson.

My parents stood locked together as one, arm and arm, both faces expressing bewilderment. Was their grandson really dead? Could he really have taken his own life? Teenagers didn't do such things when they were growing up. John's mother and stepfather stood back from the rest. Did they feel guilt on behalf of John?

O'Donnell's head was bowed, her hands folded together as the minister read a prayer. Thank God, she is able to get strength and comfort from her strong religious beliefs. She would need them. Jody was the one she had loved most in the family. He had accepted her just as she was, and he had often defended her rights to be an individual. Now he was gone. She felt alone.

Marjorie's face was tear-streaked, and behind the grief were questions she'd have to live with for a long time, perhaps forever. The two men who meant the most in her life were gone—first her father, now her brother. How could they have done this to her? Could she have stopped them if she had known what they were planning? Should she have sensed it if they were as close to her as she had thought? She felt they had let her down, and for a while it would cause her to doubt all other men.

Lisa Niner stood quietly between Marjorie and O'Donnell. There was a silent ache deep down inside her that would also last a lifetime. What if Jody had stayed with her? Maybe then we wouldn't all be standing here right now, feeling this pain. What would become of her life now that there was no hope of a renewed love between Jody and her?

Jody's other friends stood up on the hill behind the casket, next to his motorcycle—Eddie, Dean, Tommy, Doug, Ricky, and others. They all wore the same stunned expression of sadness. Young people aren't supposed to die. Teenagers are indestructible. Jody had done some pretty crazy things on a motorcycle and had never been seriously hurt. Could it really be that they would never see their friend again? How could they have known that Jody's fits of gloom could lead to this? That the drugs he had taken to make him feel better could eventually increase his depression and help bring about his death?

I had asked the minister to look toward me when he finished reading the burial service. I had told him that if I felt I could do it, there was something I wanted to say. I knew that, if God would give me the strength, there was a message I must deliver on this day to the young friends of my son who stood beside his grave.

The look came from the minister and I nodded. I would try. I stepped away from Jack and Lauren, stood beside my son, and faced the crowd. The tears started anew before I choked out my first words.

"Please bear with me. I have something I must say," I said, sobbing. I swallowed and took a deep breath. "Jody was a fine young man. You all know that." Lauren cried out loud, and Jack put his arm around her to quiet her grief. "He was a good son and brother and friend." I looked at the boys. They stared fixedly at me, waiting to hear what I had to say, almost begging for an explanation.

"He was also a terrific moto-cross racer. You guys know

that better than I do." I smiled at them through my tears. Eddie smiled back but quickly looked at the ground, seeming to be uncomfortable with a smile on that day.

"Jody would ride a good race anytime, but it was when he was behind that he rode his hardest. If he was out in front, he would cruise along with little effort. He didn't have to work very hard to stay in front. But if something happened and he got behind, if he got a bad start or he fell, that's when he would throw himself and his bike into high gear. What Jody didn't realize is that life is just like a moto-cross race. It's when you're down, when you hurt the most, that you've got to try your hardest. When you're lying on the ground, there's mud in your face, you ache all over, and every rider in the race has passed you by, that's when you have to get up, get back on that bike, and ride like hell.

"It's easy when you're out in front. No dust is being kicked up in your face, and everyone is cheering you on. It's not so easy when everything is going against you. But *that's* when you need to give it everything you've got. Jody knew that. He would never have hung it up early in a moto-cross race—not unless he was forced to." I was thinking about his last race, and it brought a new rush of tears. Why had I made him leave the track? He hadn't wanted to. I wished I hadn't insisted. I forced myself to put aside the fresh guilt and go on with what I had been saying.

"And if he didn't win that race, he knew there was always the next moto or the race next week or next year.

"Life is the same way, but Jody didn't realize it. There's always another girl, another job, another school. We shouldn't give up when we go down. We've got to get back on the bike and ride for tomorrow. Jody stopped riding, and now there are no more tomorrows, no more races to ride, no more races to be won or lost—not by Jody."

I bowed my head and let the tears flow freely. I touched the coffin and walked back to Jack's side. The service was concluded.

Jack looked over at his son. Tears were running down little Christopher's face. Jack went to him, picked him up in his arms, and held him tight. "That's all right, son," he said gently. "Go ahead and cry—cry for a boy who wasn't allowed to cry."

Jody was buried in the spring pasture of our family farm. His friends, using ropes, lowered the coffin into the ground, and then carefully shoveled in the dirt. It was one last act of friendship. It was done with the utmost love and respect. Jack stayed with the boys to help. The rest of us walked back to the house.

At the edge of the field I turned to say one more good-bye to Jody, to see Jody and his friends together for the last time. Ricky's father stood beside me. He took me in his arms and said, "Now *you* have to get back on that motorcycle."

"I know," I tried to say. The words got stuck in my throat. I tried again. "I know, and without Jody to help me." I began to sob.

EPILOGUE

*T*HERE were times when I didn't think I was going to be able to make it, to get back on the motorcycle and stay on it. I fell off a lot, but with Jack's love, understanding, and incredible patience I was able to get over the roughest spots. My daughters also gave me courage, inspiration, and reason to try to be strong.

And then there is a young man named Christopher who has a sensitivity beyond his years and a sense of humor and openness rare at any age. He is now my stepson, and he has calmed my fears about sharing another adolescent period. It *can* be different.

Also, most recently, there is a new reason for living, a new hope and promise for the future. A brand new life, a little girl named Emily, my first grandchild, the daughter of O'Donnell and Steve Timchula. A little girl who will get a lot of love and a lot of hugging from Grammie. Soon Emily will have two brothers or a brother and a sister. O'Donnell is now pregnant with twins. A sonogram shows that one of the babies is a boy; they can't tell yet about the other. *And* Marjorie and her husband, Jody Wester-lund, are expecting their first child. Four grandchildren, and I hope many more. I have a lot of love that needs to be expressed.

With the death of Jody I also discovered that I am what people call a survivor. I realized I could and would endure great pain just to be able to go on living. I recognized that even without my beloved Jody I wanted to see another summer warm the earth and make the black-eyed Susans bloom in the fields. I wanted to witness the ongoing change of seasons. I wanted to live out my life. I even wanted to grow old. There would be an empty place in my life that could never be filled, a sadness that would always be with me, just beneath the surface. But there would also be joy. I would laugh again, and I would try to bring happiness to those around me.

For people like me, who do want to live in spite of adversity, suicide is a devastating blow to what we believe in. It's hard to imagine that someone would give up on life, and if that person is someone we love, it's even harder to understand and deal with. We question what we did wrong. We question how we failed to pass on our zest for living. We question how we let that person down to the depths of self-destruction. But what we need to understand is that the human mind is as complex and as varied as there are individuals in the world and that not all are able to cope with the problems that face them in life. And that's why I encourage others not to take depression lightly. You may be someone who can overcome the down days on your own, but not everyone can.

Sometimes people need professional help to want to live. This may be especially true for troubled teenagers, whose young lives don't have the benefit of experience. A teen may have difficulty understanding that the future will bring relief and change from the pain that he or she is feeling at the moment. It's hard for a young person to realize that life can be any way other than the way it is today.

We all need help at sometime in our lives. Don't be afraid to get it for yourself or for your children. Don't do what I did and say, "Everything will eventually be all right."

It might not.

In the fall, winter, and spring of the year, when the hickory tree is not in full leaf, I can see my son's and his father's graves from my bedroom window. As I write this I can see the gravestone that marks the spot where Jody is buried. It's on the hillside in the field in back of our house. I can't read the inscription at this distance, but I know so well what it says. It is engraved in my mind as deeply as it is engraved on the white marble.

JOHN O'DONNELL WHITE, JR.

(JODY)

MARCH 8, 1960–MAY 9, 1977

HIS LIFE BROUGHT US SUCH JOY

HIS DEATH SUCH PAIN

OUR LOVE FOR HIM IS ETERNAL

I feel it could all have been so different. Jody could be alive today, an adult—well adjusted, happy, married, even providing me with additional grandchildren. I hope by sharing my pain that life can be different for you and your children. I hope that you will love one another and especially take time to say it and *show* it. Don't leave words unsaid—you may not get a second chance to say them—

and don't view teenage depression as a phase that will pass—it might not. But also remember: love is not enough.

Communicate; nothing is best left unsaid except words spoken in anger. To know what someone is thinking is to know how that person feels, and that is the first step toward understanding. We can't help each other if we don't understand each other's needs.

MYTHS ABOUT SUICIDE

FROM THE NATIONAL MENTAL HEALTH ASSOCIATION

MYTH: People who repeatedly talk about killing themselves probably won't do it.

FACT: Most people who commit suicide give definite verbal and/or behavioral warnings of their suicidal intentions. When they threaten suicide, they need help. If others ignore their talk about killing themselves, suicidal persons may actually try to commit suicide and may succeed.

MYTH: If someone really wants to kill himself or herself, there is nothing anyone can do to stop him or her.

FACT: Most people who commit suicide want desperately to live. Even the most depressed person has mixed feelings about wanting to die, sometimes wavering until the last possible moment and often giving obvious signals to others to help save him or her.

MYTH: Once a person is suicidal, he or she will always be suicidal.

FACT: The helplessness, the feeling of depression, and the thoughts about suicide last only for a limited period of time. If the suicidal or depressed person can find proper treatment during the temporary period, he or she can eventually be helped to a full, productive, and enjoyable life. Suicidal persons *can* be helped.

MYTH: Someone who seems to improve after a suicide attempt probably won't try it again.

FACT: If the conditions that caused the first attempt are not identified and dealt with, the person may find it even easier a second time. Eighty percent of all suicide victims have made one or more previous attempts. Most repeat attempts occur about three months after what seems like "improvement."

MYTH: Suicide runs in the family.

FACT: Suicidal tendencies are not inherited. However, death in the family—whether natural, accidental, or suicidal—can lead to another suicide in the family if the resulting depression from the original loss is not treated.

MYTH: Anybody who tries to kill himself or herself is basically crazy.

FACT: Although the suicidal person is extremely unhappy, he or she is not necessarily mentally ill or psychotic or insane. Most people who attempt suicide are depressed, which means they can be treated medically or psychologically. Only a few attempters can be labeled psychotic.

MYTH: The mention of suicide in front of a depressed person will give him or her suicidal ideas.

FACT: A deeply depressed person already has those ideas. You don't put the thoughts in his or her mind. By bringing up the subject you can help him or her to talk about it.

MYTH: Suicide strikes much more often among the rich— or, conversely, it occurs almost exclusively among the poor.

FACT: No single group or color or class of people is free from suicide. Rich and poor, male and female, Christian and Jew, black and white, young and old— every group is represented proportionately by suicide cases.

MYTH: Suicide happens without warning.

FACT: Studies show that most suicidal persons give many clues and signals regarding their suicidal intentions. Suicide is an act usually committed after long consideration.

ABOUT THE AUTHOR

Susan White-Bowden has been a television news reporter and anchor for WMAR-TV in Baltimore since 1967. She was the first female reporter hired at that station. The late network news anchorwoman and correspondent Jessica Savitch once referred to Susan as a pioneer in the industry, one of those who paved the way for other women in television news.

Susan has received many awards for her work, including several Associated Press awards, one for a series of reports on low-rent housing for Baltimore's poor. In 1983 Sigma Delta Chi, the Society for Professional Journalism, named her Maryland's best TV feature reporter.

Susan White-Bowden has been recognized by many for her contribution to the profession of television journalism, but she says her most important and challenging role in life has been that of a mother. "The successes are the most satisfying . . . the failures the most devastating."